I0418330

ROMANS BIBLE STUDY

A 40-DAY TRANSFORMATIVE JOURNEY
THROUGH PAUL'S MOST POWERFUL LETTER

40-DAY BIBLE STUDY SERIES
BOOK 15

PETER DEHAAN

Romans Bible Study: A 40-Day Transformative Journey Through Paul's Most Powerful Letter

Copyright © 2026 by Peter DeHaan.

40-Day Bible Study Series, Book 15

Library of Congress Control Number: 2025923631

Published by Rock Rooster Books, Grand Rapids, Michigan

ISBN:

- 979-8-88809-185-2 (ebook)
- 979-8-88809-186-9 (paperback)
- 979-8-88809-187-6 (hardcover)

Credits:

- Developmental editor: Julie Harbison
- Copyeditor: Robyn Mulder
- Cover design: Fanderclai Design
- Author photo: Chelsie Jensen Photography

To Fred Graham

Series by Peter DeHaan

40-Day Bible Study Series takes a fresh and practical look into Scripture, book by book.

Bible Character Sketches Series celebrates people in Scripture, from the well-known to the obscure.

Holiday Celebration Devotionals rejoice in the holidays with Jesus.

Visiting Churches Series takes an in-person look at church practices and traditions to inform and inspire today's followers of Jesus.

Be the first to hear about Peter's new books and receive updates at PeterDeHaan.com/updates.

CONTENTS

ROMANS

Paul, also known as Saul, wrote nearly half of the books in the New Testament, thirteen of its twenty-seven sections. Beyond that, the content of his writing comprises about one third of the New Testament text. This makes Paul the leading contributor to the Bible's New Testament. As a result, his writing was most influential to Jesus's church then, which continues through to us today.

The New Testament contains multiple genres of writing. It opens with four biographies of Jesus, then chronicles the history of the early church, and ends with John's epic vision. The rest of the New Testament books are letters, also called epistles. All of Paul's writing are letters to various churches or individuals.

On Paul's second missionary journey, he visited many of the cities that he later wrote letters to. This includes Corinth, Galatia, Ephesus, Philippi, and Thessalonica. Though he wrote letters to the churches in Colossae and Rome, he hadn't gone to either city.

Even though Paul has never visited the church in Rome, he has heard about them. He writes that their faith is reported all over the world. Paul prays for them, longs to see them, and even planned to visit them, but couldn't do so (Romans 1:8–13). He also says everyone has heard about their obedience (Romans 16:19).

It's from this perspective that Paul pens his letter to them.

Romans is an epistle to Gentile believers in Rome, and by extension the Roman Empire (the dominant world power of the day), which was the same as writing to the entire known world at that time.

The book of Romans is an organized summary of Paul's message, which is found scattered throughout his other writings. It's an esteemed and profoundly influential letter that lays out the importance and significance of salvation through Jesus.

As such, its focus is on the fundamentals of theology. But don't let the word *theology* scare you away. The basic understanding of theology is to study the nature of God and his truth. Romans does an excellent job in accomplishing this.

Here's a basic outline of our journey through the book of Romans:

- **Days 1–11: Faith Foundations (Romans 1–5)** looks at the gospel's power, sin's presence, and justification by faith, as demonstrated through Abraham.
- **Days 12–20: Freedom from Sin (Romans 6–8)** considers what baptism symbolizes, struggles with sin, Holy Spirit empowerment, and our future with God.
- **Days 21–27: God's Plan for All (Romans 9–11)** covers Israel's role, faith over law, and God's grace and mercy for both Jews and Gentiles.
- **Days 28–40: Living the Faith (Romans 12–16)** addresses living

sacrificially, putting love into action, Christian unity, and Paul's mission, before ending with a long list of people to greet. This section is reminiscent of Proverbs with its concise listings of commands, instructions, and advice.

As you read Romans chapters one through eleven, watch for ideas that repeat, with slight variation. Repetition was a common practice at the time to draw attention to important concepts. Be sure not to miss them.

Until now, what has been your view of the book of Romans? What do you think about the word theology? *Given the information in this introduction, what do you hope to gain from this study? Do you expect it will help you mature in your faith?*

[Discover more about maturing in our faith in Hebrews 6:1–2.]

DAY 1: A SERVANT OF JESUS
ROMANS 1:1–7

Paul, a servant of Christ Jesus, called to be an apostle and set apart for the gospel of God. (Romans 1:1)

Paul opens his letter to the Romans with a lengthy salutation. It's the longest greeting in any of his letters, clocking in at seven verses. It's not until the last verse that we know who he's writing to. The first six are about himself.

In doing so, Paul establishes credibility for his message, which encourages his recipients to take his words seriously. But the attributes also seem like a mini-biography, one with spiritual importance.

Here is Paul's threefold self-assessment in the opening verse:

A Servant of Jesus: Personally, I prefer to call myself a follower of Jesus—as opposed to the more general description of Christian, which means different things to different people. Being a follower of Jesus shows commitment, yet it still implies I have some say in the matter, that I made a choice.

Being a servant, however, carries with it a much deeper commitment. We must move our mindsets from being a follower to voluntarily becoming his servant. This makes Jesus our master. We must therefore be faithful servants and do what he says—all of it.

Called to Be an Apostle: Instead of focusing on the word *apostle*, which could suggest a missionary, a church leader, or a passionate adherent (all of which describe Paul), let's instead focus on the word *called*. What does it mean to be called by God?

While we may not have a calling at the same high level as Paul, all Christians are called, first to follow Jesus (as in "Come, follow me," Matthew 4:19) and then to obey him (John 8:51).

As we serve him, he will tell us to do other things too. These are our callings, even if we're not traveling around the world as his missionaries.

Set Apart for the Gospel: While being set apart could be a Spirit-led summoning of the highest order (Acts 13:2), it could also be a simple command to set ourselves apart from the world, to not be conformed to it (Romans 12:2). Everyone who follows Jesus should be set apart in this way, while being open for him to also set us apart for something greater.

If we are a true Christian (as opposed to being one in name only), we will do well to adopt the attitude of Paul: that through Jesus we are his servants, called, and set apart.

Do we act like Jesus's servants? What are we called to do for him? How do we live as set apart for the gospel?

[Discover five more servants of Jesus in Philippians 1:1, Colossians 4:12, James 1:1, 2 Peter 1:1, and Jude 1:1.]

DAY 2: NOT ASHAMED
ROMANS 1:8–17

For I am not ashamed of the gospel, because it is the power of God that brings salvation to everyone who believes: first to the Jew, then to the Gentile. (Romans 1:16)

By the time we get to today's focus verse, Paul has already used the word *gospel* four times in his letter. And he'll use it several more times before he finishes. In simple terms, the gospel of Jesus means the good news about him. Jesus came to earth to save us. This is indeed good news—the greatest news of all time.

Paul has already stated that he has been set apart to share the gospel—the good news about

Jesus's salvation—with others, specifically the Gentiles. This means everyone who's not Jewish.

Given that Paul is a servant of Jesus, called and set apart to tell others about him, it seems strange that he feels the need to assert that he is not ashamed. With all Paul has done for Jesus, the many ways he has suffered (2 Corinthians 11:16–33), and his bold declarations (Acts 13:46, Acts 14:3, Acts 19:8, and Acts 28:30–31) it's clear he's not ashamed. Yet Paul proclaims to the Romans that he is not ashamed of Jesus's good news.

We may think of being ashamed as being embarrassed or fearful. When we talk to others about Jesus, they may laugh at us, they may verbally attack us, or they may mock our faith. Even more so, we could suffer persecution for spreading the good news about Jesus.

But *not ashamed* could also mean a lack of reluctance. It could suggest a willingness or openness. Consider the book of Hebrews. The writers say that Jesus is not ashamed to call us brothers and sisters (Hebrews 2:11). He is willing and open to do so, perhaps even eager. His not being ashamed of us emerges as a comforting embrace.

Later, in Hebrews 11, which some people call the Hall of Faith, we read about some patriarchs—

Abel, Enoch, Noah, Abraham, Issac, and Jacob—and their faithfulness to God. Because of their confidence in him and their eternal perspective, God is not ashamed to be called their God (Hebrews 11:16).

When we put our faith in Jesus and are made right with Father God, he likewise is not ashamed to be called our God.

If God is not ashamed to be our God, we should certainly not be ashamed of him or his Son.

Are we embarrassed because we follow Jesus? Are we fearful of what others may say or do when we talk about him? What do we think about Jesus and Father God not being ashamed of us?

[Discover another person who was not ashamed in 2 Timothy 1:16.]

DAY 3: GOD'S WRATH
ROMANS 1:18–32

The wrath of God is being revealed from heaven against all the godlessness and wickedness of people, who suppress the truth by their wickedness. (Romans 1:18)

M any people see God as a loving God. He is. Therefore, the idea of his wrath seems counter to his character. Yet both his love and his wrath are part of who he is.

What's the source of God's wrath? It's people who are godless and evil, suppressing his truth with their wickedness. They have every reason to know him (Romans 2:14–15). But they choose not to. They think they're wise, but this only reveals their foolishness. They turn to idolatry. In doing so, they earn God's wrath.

Because of this, God gave them over to their hearts' sinful desires to pursue sexual impurity with each other. We need not wonder what sexual impurity is. Paul details it. Sexual impurity is women who exchange heterosexual sex for unnatural pursuits. It's men who replace their created desire for women with lust for other men. In short, it's homosexuality.

Though many people today embrace homosexuality as both permissible and acceptable, God has a different perspective. God created us as male and female, giving us the command to be fruitful and multiply. He first told this to Adam and Eve (Genesis 1:26–28). He later repeated it to Noah (Genesis 9:7).

Also, the Old Testament law tells the people who not to have sex with (Leviticus 18:6–24 and Leviticus 20:13). Now Paul confirms God's intended order. God does not change, and neither do his expectations for his creation.

Yet some today decry this idea of sexual impurity as outdated, even labeling those who proclaim God's truth as engaging in hate speech. Yet is it hateful to tell others that their sin pulls them away from God and the potential of spending eternity with him? No. Speaking godly truth is love, not hate.

People who advocate lifestyles contrary to what God teaches haven't read the Bible—or they don't believe what it says. Perhaps they simply choose to disregard the sections that confront the lifestyle they want to live. Or maybe they try to twist the passages they don't believe in so that they better align with how they act—or at least so they don't confront it.

Regardless, if we think God reserves his wrath for homosexuals, Paul follows this with a slew of other sinful traits: every kind of wickedness, evil, greed, and depravity. First, they're full of envy, murder, strife, deceit, and malice. They gossip, slander, and hate God. And they're insolent, arrogant, and boastful. Beyond that, they invent ways of doing evil, disobey their parents, and have no understanding, no fidelity, no love, and no mercy. Not only do they do these things, but they encourage others to do so as well (Romans 1:29–32).

In doing this, they earn God's wrath.

How do we balance God's love with his wrath? Given what the Bible teaches, what should be our view of homosexuality? What do we think about the other traits on Paul's lengthy list? How willing are we to speak God's truth to others who may not want to hear it?

[Discover more about sexual impurity in 2 Corinthians 12:21, Galatians 5:19, Ephesians 5:3, and Colossians 3:5. Read what else Paul says about this topic in 1 Corinthians 6:9–11 and 1 Timothy 1:8–11.]

DAY 4: JUDGE NOT
ROMANS 2:1–16

You, therefore, have no excuse, you who pass judgment on someone else, for at whatever point you judge another, you are condemning yourself, because you who pass judgment do the same things. (Romans 2:1)

Yesterday's reading about sexual impurity isn't the concluding thought on the subject. Today's passage builds on the discussion, bringing us to a fuller comprehension. We know this because today's verse, which opens the passage, contains the transitional word *therefore*. This one word reminds us to connect what precedes it with what follows. Doing so will allow us to better understand the passage we're exploring.

In view of the sinful traits Paul lists in the preceding passage, we have no excuse. We know what is right and should do it. We know what is wrong and should avoid it. This includes homosexuality, along with all the other sins Paul lists. Yet too often we're quick to pass judgment on those whom we deem to have fallen short.

We live in a polarized society with divisive points of view. We perceive people from this perspective. There are those who agree with us and then there's everyone else. We reason that we're right, and they're wrong. We judge them as lacking.

Yet Paul reminds us that we struggle in our behavior too. It's wrong for us to condemn others when we do—or may do—the same things.

In Jesus's two longest sermons, he tells the crowd (and us) not to judge others. If we do, we will likewise face judgment. In his Sermon on the Mount, Jesus adds that as we measure others, so too will we be measured (Matthew 7:1–2). And in his Sermon on the Plain, Jesus adds that if we don't condemn others, we will not be condemned either. If we forgive others, we will be forgiven (Luke 6:37). Therefore, don't judge, don't condemn, and be quick to forgive.

Yet there may be an exception.

Paul had told the church in Corinth not to associate with sexually immoral people (1 Corinthians 5:1–13). He clarifies he didn't mean immoral people in the world.

His command specifically addressed people within the church. This means those who claim to be a brother and sister through Jesus while persisting in sexual immorality, as well as greed, idolatry, slander, drunkenness, and swindling.

Paul tells them not even to eat with such people. Though Paul will not judge those outside the church, he will judge those on the inside. Let God judge those who aren't in the church, but we should judge those who are within it. In this case, Paul tells them to expel the wicked person from within.

Yet the judgment Paul authorizes on the man who committed sexual immorality was not permanent. It was temporary. After the man's implicit repentance, Paul tells the Corinthians to welcome him back and reaffirm their love for him (2 Corinthians 2:6–8).

Though we should not judge the world, perhaps we need to do a better job of judging the church, including those engaged in sexual immorality.

How quick are we to judge those we disagree with? Are we quicker to condemn others or forgive them? What is our view of sin in the world? What is our view of sin within Jesus's church?

[Discover more about judgment in 1 Corinthians 4:3–5, Colossians 2:16, Hebrews 13:4, and James 4:11–12.]

BONUS CONTENT: THEREFORE

Therefore, the promise comes by faith. (Romans 4:16)

W e've already encountered the word *therefore* in Romans. It will pop up a total of twenty-one times. A clever study aid is that whenever we see the word *therefore*, we must look at what it's *there for*. This means letting the text that precedes this pivotal word inform what follows it.

Here are the twenty-one verses in Romans that contain *therefore*. To best understand the context of these verses will, of course, require looking at the passage that precedes each one to see what it's there for:

1. Romans 1:24: "Therefore God gave them over in the sinful desires of their hearts."
2. Romans 2:1: "You, therefore, have no excuse, you who pass judgment on someone else."
3. Romans 3:20: "Therefore no one will be declared righteous in God's sight by the works of the law."
4. Romans 4:16: "Therefore, the promise comes by faith."
5. Romans 5:1: "Therefore, since we have been justified through faith, we have peace with God through our Lord Jesus Christ."
6. Romans 5:12: "Therefore, just as sin entered the world through one man, and death through sin . . ."
7. Romans 6:4: "We were therefore buried with him through baptism into death."
8. Romans 6:12: "Therefore do not let sin reign in your mortal body."
9. Romans 8:1: "Therefore, there is now no condemnation for those who are in Christ Jesus."

10. Romans 8:12: "Therefore, brothers and sisters, we have an obligation—but it is not to the flesh."

11. Romans 9:16: "It does not, therefore, depend on human desire or effort, but on God's mercy."

12. Romans 9:18: "Therefore God has mercy on whom he wants to have mercy, and he hardens whom he wants to harden."

13. Romans 11:22: "Consider therefore the kindness and sternness of God."

14. Romans 12:1: "Therefore . . . offer your bodies as a living sacrifice."

15. Romans 13:5: "Therefore, it is necessary to submit to the authorities, not only because of possible punishment but also as a matter of conscience."

16. Romans 13:10: "Therefore love is the fulfillment of the law."

17. Romans 14:13: "Therefore let us stop passing judgment on one another."

18. Romans 14:16: "Therefore do not let what you know is good be spoken of as evil."

19. Romans 14:19: "Let us therefore make every effort to do what leads to peace."
20. Romans 15:9: "As it is written: 'Therefore I will praise you among the Gentiles.'"
21. Romans 15:17: "Therefore I glory in Christ Jesus in my service to God."

In case you're wondering, *therefore* occurs in most of the books in the Bible (442 verses) and more often in Romans than any other New Testament book.

Which of the above verses do you want to investigate more fully? What other verses can you think of that have the word therefore*?*

[Discover times when Jesus used *therefore* in Luke 7:47, Luke 8:18, Luke 11:36, and Luke 12:22, along with many more.]

DAY 5: TEACH YOURSELVES
ROMANS 2:17–29

You, then, who teach others, do you not teach yourself? You who preach against stealing, do you steal? (Romans 2:21)

As Paul continues his letter, he has some critical words for teachers. He implies they're hypocritical. They must examine themselves, therefore, to make sure that they do not do the very things they tell others not to do.

If we know we shouldn't steal, but steal anyway, that's bad. But if we tell others—that is, if we teach them—not to steal, and then steal anyway, it's much worse.

Because of these teachers' double standards, those outside the church blaspheme God's name.

How terrible! Not only do these teachers harm their students, they also damage Jesus's reputation before a world that desperately needs to hear about his truth and salvation.

We've all encountered people like this. They gush at length about their faith, but their lives don't back it up. Their actions besmirch the name of Jesus. They don't draw others to him. Instead, they drive people away.

Jesus also addressed misguided teachers and called them hypocrites. Their error was going to great lengths to convert one person and then teaching them the wrong things, thereby making their situation even worse (Matthew 23:15).

In this letter, Paul had earlier criticized people who do what is wrong, as well as those who approve of their actions (Romans 1:32). This sounds a lot like teachers who tell people it's okay for them to sin. But sin has no place in our lives as followers of Jesus (Romans 6:1–2).

It's critical for teachers to align their behavior with their words. It's also essential that their teaching encourages people to improve their behavior and not accomplish the opposite.

Given the important role teachers play, James advises that few of us should aspire to be teachers.

This is because teachers face higher expectations and will be judged more strictly when they fall short (James 3:1).

Yet, we're wrong to assume we should avoid being teachers simply because of the higher standards we're called to. Instead, when we teach each other—either formally or informally—we should strive to do so with integrity. We should make every effort to ensure our lifestyle matches what we tell others to do and what we expect of them.

In what ways do we teach others? What behavior must we change to make sure our teachings aren't hypocritical? What can we do to better align our words with our actions? How can we best point people to Jesus?

[Discover passages about false teachers in 1 Timothy 1:3–4, 1 Timothy 6:3–5, 2 Timothy 2:14–18, and 2 Peter 2:1–3. Read about the qualifications for overseers and elders—both of whom serve as teachers—in 1 Timothy 3:1–7 and Titus 1:5–9.]

DAY 6: A CHOSEN PEOPLE

ROMANS 3:1–8

The Jews have been entrusted with the very words of God.
(Romans 3:2)

C hapter 2 of the book of Romans ends with a discussion about the law, which details the important rite of circumcision (Romans 2:25–29). According to the law, all male Jews would be circumcised as infants. This was a physical sign that they were God's people.

Yet many who did this rite did so with legalistic obligation. Though they were outwardly Jews—in a physical sense—they were not inwardly Jews from a spiritual perspective. It's what was in their hearts that mattered. It's following the spirit of the law and not the letter. For circumcision to have any real importance, it must be regarded with intention and not casual indifference.

The implication is that not all Jews are truly Jewish. Conversely, some non-Jews can become spiritually Jewish. In God's eyes, ethnicity doesn't seem to matter.

With this as our background, we slide into chapter 3. Not surprisingly, Paul asks a rhetorical question: "Is there any advantage to being Jewish?"

Given what Paul has just said, we might assume the answer is no. Yet he is not willing to dismiss his Jewish people and their ancestors. He says there is a significant advantage in being Jewish. This is because the Jews have been entrusted with God's very words.

Without God's words, as recorded in the Old Testament, we would not have the law, which proves the need for a better way to be saved. We would also not have the prophets' words that point to a coming Savior who will save both Jew and Gentile alike. And without the Jews, we would not have Jesus—for Jesus is a Jew.

In short, God's words have come to us through the Jews, God's chosen people. He selected them to be a holy people out of all the nations of the world. He treasures them as his own (Deuteronomy 7:6).

Yet birthright alone does not guarantee the Jews their salvation. Some were unfaithful, yet God stands by them anyway. He remains faithful to them, even though they were not faithful to him.

May we today—both Jew and Gentile—remain faithful to God.

What should our attitude be toward Jewish people? What do we think about Jesus being Jewish? How can we remain faithful to God today?

[Discover what Isaiah says about God's chosen people in Isaiah 43:19–21, Isaiah 65:9, and Isaiah 65:22. Read how Paul and Peter expand on this idea of God's chosen people in Colossians 3:12 and 1 Peter 2:4–9.]

DAY 7: THE LAW REVEALS SIN
ROMANS 3:9–20

Therefore no one will be declared righteous in God's sight by the works of the law; rather, through the law we become conscious of our sin. (Romans 3:20)

We rightly think of the law as being an Old Testament concept. Yet the New Testament mentions *the law* more than twice as much as the Old Testament. Even more interesting is that Paul talks about the law in Romans more than in any other book in the Bible.

The Old Testament law revealed God's expectations for his people. But it wasn't just the Ten Commandments. It was a far more expansive list.

Old Testament scholars count 613 such laws—that is, rules—for the people to follow. This told the Hebrews, in painstaking detail, what to do and what not to do.

By obeying all these rules, they would become righteous before God. But no one could keep the entire set of laws. It was impossible. As a result, no one could be declared righteous merely by following the law—because they couldn't. This meant that before God, everyone failed. They were, in fact, unrighteous. The law proved it. In this way, the law confirmed that no one could ever please God.

If the law failed to make us right, what purpose did it serve? Was it simply to present an impossible standard for the people to follow, one which would doom them for eternity?

No. The purpose of the law was to reveal our sinful nature.

When Adam and Eve disobeyed God in the garden of Eden by eating from the one forbidden tree, they allowed sin to enter our world. As a result, this opened all their descendants to the bondage of sin as well. Through one man, Adam, sin entered our world. Through another man, Jesus, God provides for our rescue from sin. (Paul expands on this later in his letter and we'll cover that in Day 12.)

If the purpose of the law wasn't to save us, but merely to make us aware of sin, then why do many people today try to approach God by following a bunch of rules? It makes no sense. But they try to do it anyway. They think they can earn their salvation.

Many people today persist in the fallacy that if they're mostly good, this will please God. Then they'll go to heaven when they die. They wrongly view their lifetime of actions as placed on a balance scale. If they pile up more good things on one side than bad things on the other, the balance will tip in their favor. Then, they will please God, and he will accept them.

Yet, as we will soon learn, we can't earn our salvation by following a set of rules, neither the ones in the Bible nor the ones we make up.

Fortunately, the solution is much simpler. We'll cover this in the next chapter.

How should we rightly view the Old Testament law? What is our attitude toward sin? How might we be trying to earn our salvation? What rules do we persist in following today?

[Discover more about the law in 1 Timothy 1:9–11.]

DAY 8: JUSTIFIED BY FAITH
ROMANS 3:21–31

For we maintain that a person is justified by faith apart from the works of the law. (Romans 3:28)

We said that Paul talks about the *law* in his letter to the Romans more than in any other book of the Bible. Interestingly—and appropriately so—Paul uses the word *justify* a lot in this letter too. Justify occurs more in Romans than in any other book in the Bible. The two words go together. The law reveals our sin, and we are justified by faith. We need the former to make way for the latter.

Since the law can't save us and was merely to

reveal our sin, there must be a better way. And God planned to provide this superior approach from the very beginning. After all, Adam and Eve's sin did not surprise him.

The Old Testament prophets foresaw this better solution to the problem of sin. It was a coming Messiah who would rescue the people. This Savior would save the people from their sins, thereby making them right with Father God.

As God's chosen people, the Jews assumed this promised Messiah would be only for them. But God had a more inclusive plan, which embraced everyone. Therefore, through Jesus, both Jew and Gentile can be saved.

All that's needed is faith. By faith we are justified—that is, we're made right with Father God. This occurs apart from the law and not through it. When God justifies us through faith, it frees us from the guilt of sin and the penalty our sins deserve. It's just as if we had never sinned.

Through faith we are justified and saved from our sin and its consequences.

Once, when Jesus is teaching the people, someone asks if only a few will be saved. His answer is both surprising and comforting (Luke 13:22–30).

Jesus implores his listeners—who were all Jewish—to make every effort to enter through the narrow door. He warns them that many will try to enter and fail.

Why is this?

It could be because they'll try to enter based on their legalistic efforts to follow the law. But the law can't save them. Only faith in Jesus can. Jesus is the gate to salvation (John 10:9). He is the way, the only way (John 14:6).

We may be surprised, and perhaps discouraged, that many will not be saved, but remember this refers to those—both the Jew and non-Jew—who try to earn their salvation by following a list of rules.

But for all others, the door is wide open. People will flock from every direction—east, west, north, and south—to take their place in God's kingdom. For them, the path is easy because they are justified by their faith.

Faith is the key that opens the door.

Do we rely on our faith alone to save us? How should we react to people who try to earn their salvation instead of being justified by faith? What should we do when people insist we follow their religious rules?

[Discover more about being justified in 1 Corinthians 6:11, Galatians 2:15–16, and Titus 3:4–7.]

BONUS CONTENT: ROMAN'S ROAD

For all have sinned and fall short of the glory of God.
(Romans 3:23)

Have you ever heard of the Roman's Road? This doesn't refer to a physical path, but a spiritual one. It's based on Paul's teachings in his letter to the Romans. It's a series of verses that easily explain God's plan of salvation through Jesus (and not the law).

Here are the key verses that comprise the Roman's Road:

- Romans 3:23: Everyone does wrong

things—we sin—and fall short of God's expectations.

- Romans 6:23: Though we deserve the death penalty for our sins, God gives us eternal life through Jesus.
- Romans 5:8: Because God loves us so much, he sent Jesus to die in our place for our sins.
- Romans 10:9–10: All we need to do is declare that Jesus is Lord and believe that God raised him from the dead.
- Romans 10:13: When we do this, we will be saved. It's that simple.

(Some people add Romans 5:1, Romans 5:12, and Romans 8:1 to this list, which provide additional insights that build upon the five essential verses.)

How do these verses encourage us on our faith journey? Who do we need to share them with?

[Discover more about salvation in Romans 8:38–39.]

Have you declared Jesus as your Lord and believed that God raised him from the dead? If not, will you do so today? Your future with Jesus awaits.

DAY 9: ABRAHAM'S FAITH
ROMANS 4:1–15

We have been saying that Abraham's faith was credited to him as righteousness. (Romans 4:9)

I n his letter to the Romans, Paul works hard to let his audience know, without a doubt, that it was Abraham's faith that saved him and not anything he had done. Paul reiterates this truth to make sure we don't miss it.

As a result, God gave Abraham the rite of circumcision. It's important to realize—and embrace—that Abraham's circumcision came *after* his faith was credited to him as righteousness and not before.

As such, circumcision was not a prerequisite for

Abraham to earn God's attention. Instead, circumcision was a reaction to what God had already done for the patriarch. Circumcision was the result of Abraham's right standing with God. It wasn't a prelude to receiving God's affirmation.

Over four centuries later, along comes Moses. Moses delivers the people out of their slavery in Egypt. Before they head to the land God promised for them to receive, he gives Moses the law. This includes the Ten Commandments and the other rules and expectations God has for his people. The purpose is to teach them what to do and not to do.

This means that Abraham didn't have the law to follow when he was alive. Yet even though the law didn't exist for him, God didn't require Abraham to work to earn his righteousness. That is, to achieve his right standing with God. Instead, Abraham received it through faith. Abraham's faith was credited to him as righteousness. David later confirms that this concept continues for the people even after God gave them his law (Psalm 32:1–2).

As Jesus's followers today, we don't have the religious rite of circumcision in our faith practices. But we have baptism. Just as circumcision was not a requirement for Abraham but a response to his already established faith, so, too, is baptism for us today. We don't need to be baptized to be right with Father God. Instead, we accept Jesus through faith. Then we are baptized in response to what he has already done for us.

Just as circumcision was an outward sign of Abraham's right standing with God, so, too, is baptism an outward sign—a public display—of our right standing with God, one that we have already received.

Neither circumcision nor baptism saves us. Only Jesus can do that. We need to accept him by faith. It's that simple.

What role does baptism play in our faith journey today? How should we react to people who have a different view of baptism than ours? How should we view others who follow Jesus but haven't been baptized?

[Discover more about Abraham's faith in Hebrews 11:8–19. Read Stephen's summary of Abraham's life in Acts 7:2–8.]

DAY 10: THE ENTIRE
WORLD IS BLESSED
ROMANS 4:16–25

[Jesus] was delivered over to death for our sins and was raised to life for our justification. (Romans 4:25)

Today's passage opens with the connecting word *therefore*. As we look at what it's there for, we investigate what precedes it to inform what follows it.

The preceding passage talks about the promise God makes to Abraham, that Abraham would be heir of the world.

What does it mean that Abraham will be heir of the world? It likely refers to all peoples on earth (Genesis 12:3) and all nations (Genesis 18:18 and

Genesis 22:18). This is because through Abraham, all the world will be blessed. In this way, he is our father, and we are his heirs.

But God's promise to Abraham—and our blessing—is not through the law (which God will later give to Moses) but through faith. Abraham was made righteous through faith. So are we.

But how can Abraham be the father of many nations when he and his wife, Sarah, have no children? This presents quite a dilemma. Yet against all hope, Abraham believes.

Over the years, Abraham and Sarah grow older, yet they remain childless. Abraham perseveres in faith. At last, when he is one hundred years old and Sarah is ninety, they have Isaac. Isaac is the father of Jacob (later called Israel). Jacob has twelve sons. They become the twelve tribes of Israel and grow to become the nation of Israel.

Several centuries after Abraham, we have Moses and after that, King David. We then have the prophets, such as Isaiah. They are all offspring of Abraham, the result of God's improbable promise to the patriarch.

The most noteworthy descendant of Abraham, however, is Jesus. Yes, Jesus is a direct descendant of Abraham (Matthew 1:1–16).

As we mentioned in Day 7, the law reveals our sinful nature. Our sin makes us fall short of Father God's expectations. We miss the mark. We deserve the death penalty for all our mistakes.

Jesus came to earth to sacrifice himself on our behalf. He died so we wouldn't have to. This great gift to us doesn't end with his execution. His crucifixion was just the beginning. Jesus overcame the finality of the tomb and rose from the dead. He defeated death. By overcoming the grave, all who believe in Jesus will be justified. That is, we will be made right with Papa. Then, we too will overcome death through our belief in Jesus.

In this way, we see God's promise of blessing the entire world through Abraham coming to fruition through Jesus's saving power brought on by his death and resurrection. Jesus died so that we might live forever with him. Everyone—all the people of the earth and all nations—who puts their faith in Jesus can likewise live with him forever. In this way, the entire world is blessed.

What do we think about Jesus dying for our sins so that we don't have to? How does Jesus's resurrection from the dead encourage us in the eternal life we will receive after our bodies die? How can Abraham's life encourage us to be a blessing to others?

[Discover more about Abraham's story in Genesis 17:1–22, Genesis 18:9–15 and Genesis 21:1–6.]

DAY 11: THE BENEFITS OF SUFFERING
ROMANS 5:1–11

We also glory in our sufferings, because we know that suffering produces perseverance; perseverance, character; and character, hope. (Romans 5:3–4)

Today's passage continues and builds upon the prior text in Paul's letter, which we covered in Day 10. As a result, our faith in Jesus's saving power justifies us in God's sight; our Savior makes us right in our Heavenly Father's eyes. Because of this, we stand firm in his grace. Then we can boast in our hope—our expectation—of one day being in God's glory. What a magnificent promise to anticipate.

Not only do we look forward to the glory of

God, but we can also glory in our sufferings. But why would we want to do that? Suffering occurs because of pain, misery, or loss. Why would we want to glory in these things? Being in God's glory is positive, while the thought of glorying in our suffering seems negative—even foolhardy.

We can think of this glory as rejoicing in triumph and in exultation. Yet we again wonder, why would we want to rejoice in and exult over our pain, misery, and loss?

There are many ways we can suffer. We can suffer physically and spiritually. We can also suffer mentally and emotionally. And we bring some suffering upon ourselves because of our bad choices. Others inflict suffering on us. As followers of Jesus, people may persecute us. In fact, we should expect it. When this happens, we suffer.

But why should we glory in our sufferings? Because of what our suffering produces—at least when we suffer in a God-honoring way.

When we respond rightly to our sufferings, we produce perseverance. We don't give up. We press on amid our distress. With God's provision and grace, we move through our suffering.

As we persevere, we grow stronger. Our character matures. The result is increased ways to serve him. There's more we can do to grow the kingdom of God. And there's more we can do to reach the lost and encourage the saints.

Finally, from our character comes hope. We hope for the future. Although we may not always realize the future we hope for in this world, we will certainly realize a glorious future in the next.

Regardless of the sufferings we endure today, we have confidence we will spend eternity with Father God and Jesus. Today's suffering means nothing compared with our future glory (Romans 8:18).

What is our first reaction to suffering? Should we try to avoid suffering for Jesus? In what ways has our suffering produced perseverance in us? How has our character grown because of it?

[Discover more about suffering in 2 Corinthians 1:5–7, Ephesians 3:13, and 2 Timothy 1:8.]

BONUS CONTENT: GRACE

We have peace with God through our Lord Jesus Christ,
through whom we have gained access by faith into this grace
in which we now stand. (Romans 5:1–2)

P aul talks a lot about grace in this letter.
The word appears eighteen times in
Romans, more than in any other book of
the Bible.

Grace is a word we say often and with ease. Yet
what exactly does it mean? One definition of grace
is "favor given by someone who doesn't have to
offer it." This is how Scripture often uses the word
grace.

Though God doesn't have to grant us his favor, he does. It's a sign of how much he loves us.

The dictionary definition is most helpful, but I prefer a more succinct explanation that relates directly to God and us: Grace is getting good things that we don't deserve.

Though people sometimes use grace and mercy interchangeably, think of mercy as not getting the bad things that we deserve. As such, grace and mercy work in tandem, offering us a powerful understanding of just how much God loves us. (Not surprisingly, Paul also mentions mercy often in this letter, with only the book of Psalms surpassing it.)

It's by God's grace that we are saved, which we receive through faith. It's a gift from God and nothing we can earn (Ephesians 2:8–9).

Thank you, Jesus, for offering us your grace.

How should we react to receiving God's grace? How should we react to receiving God's mercy?

[Discover more about grace in John 1:17, Acts 15:11, Galatians 1:6–7, and 2 Thessalonians 2:16–17.]

DAY 12: ADAM AND JESUS
ROMANS 5:12–21

Just as one trespass resulted in condemnation for all people, so also one righteous act resulted in justification and life for all people. (Romans 5:18)

I n the beginning of our world, God places Adam and Eve in an idyllic paradise, the garden of Eden. He tells Adam he can eat from any tree in the garden, except for one: the tree of the knowledge of good and evil. If he eats its fruit, he will die (Genesis 2:16–17).

In this garden paradise, a crafty serpent comes to Eve. He questions God's command. He tells her God is wrong, that eating from the tree will not bring about death. Instead, it will make them more like God; their eyes would open, and they would know both good and evil.

Eve knew what God had told Adam, but she disregards God's words and believes the serpent's lie. She eats the tree's fruit. She gives some to Adam, and he eats it too. Their eyes are indeed opened. They see they're naked and are ashamed (Genesis 3:1–7).

Though they do not immediately die, they do, in fact, one day perish. Their sin results in their death. So too for all their descendants. So too for us today. Our sin results in our death.

We might blame Eve for this. She believed the serpent's lie, ate the fruit first, and then talked Adam into eating it. Yet, Paul places the blame on Adam.

When Adam (and Eve) believed the serpent's lie instead of God's truth and acted upon it, they invited sin into the world. Sin has reigned here ever since, and with sin comes death.

God later gives Adam and Eve's descendants the law. As we saw in Day 7, the purpose of the law is to reveal our sinful nature. In the Old Testament, the temporary solution to sin is an annual animal sacrifice. Yet this must be repeated year after year, century after century. It seems futile.

Yet God provides a better way. It's through Jesus. Jesus comes to earth and dies as the ultimate sin sacrifice. His death covers all the sins, of all people, throughout all time. Through Jesus we have a permanent solution to the problem of sin and death. Through Jesus we can have the penalty of our sins washed away. Then we can live *for* him now and *with* him forever in eternity.

Just as sin and death entered the world through one man, Adam, sin and death are likewise overcome by one man, Jesus.

To make sure we don't miss this, Paul repeats it. He introduces the idea in verse 12, expands on it in verse 15, and reiterates it three times in verses 17, 18, and 19.

Through Adam and Eve, we have sin and death. Through Jesus we have righteousness and life.

How do we view Adam and Eve for eating the forbidden fruit? What is our view of sin and death? What can we do to better embrace righteousness and life through Jesus?

[Discover more about eternal life through Jesus in John 3:14–18, 1 Timothy 1:16, and 1 John 5:11.]

DAY 13: ALIVE IN JESUS
ROMANS 6:1–14

In the same way, count yourselves dead to sin but alive to God in Christ Jesus. (Romans 6:11)

The rite of baptism doesn't show up in the Bible until we get to the New Testament. It begins with John the baptizer, who submerges people in the Jordan River as a sign of repentance. Jesus's disciples likewise baptize those who repent from their wrong way of life and make a U-turn to follow him. Today, Jesus's followers continue the practice of baptism as a public display of their faith.

One way to view baptism is as a symbolic

washing of our sins to make us clean and justified before our Heavenly Father.

Another visual sees baptism as a powerful symbol that shows Jesus's death, burial, and resurrection. Think of these three words while envisioning immersion baptism. Going into the water represents death, being submerged represents burial, and emerging from the water represents resurrection.

We are wise to embrace both perspectives. Baptism shows us being cleansed through Jesus, as well as dying and resurrecting with him.

Paul's letter to the Romans focuses on the idea of baptism signifying death, burial, and resurrection.

When we're baptized, we affiliate with Jesus and what he did for us. Our baptism shows we align with his death and are resurrected to live a new life. We unite with him in death, and we unite with him in resurrection.

In the symbolism of death that going into the water shows, we see our old, sinful self being crucified with him. Sin no longer rules over us. We are no longer slaves to it. Our figurative death through Jesus sets us free from sin.

Yet not only do we die with Jesus, we will also

resurrect with him. Jesus overcame death when he rose to life anew from his grave. He was victorious over death, and it no longer controls him. He lives, and he lives his life to please God. So should we.

Through Jesus—as shown through baptism—we should deem ourselves dead to sin and alive to our Heavenly Father.

This doesn't mean we'll never sin again. It means we need to change our perspective of sin. We mustn't let sin rule us. We need to stop obeying evil desires. In this way, we shouldn't let any part of our being be a tool for evil. Instead, we should strive to be instruments of righteousness.

We should not let sin be our master. Instead, we can align with Paul and view ourselves as servants of Jesus (Romans 1:1).

What does our baptism mean to us? What should our attitude be toward sin? Are we willing to be a servant of Jesus?

[Discover more about baptism in Matthew 28:18–20, Luke 3:16, and Colossians 2:11–12.]

BONUS CONTENT: BY NO MEANS

Shall we go on sinning so that grace may increase? By no means! (Romans 6:1–2)

Paul wraps up Romans chapter 5 with a reminder that the purpose of the law was to reveal our sin, so that our trespass might increase. Yet this shouldn't concern us, because when sin increases, God's grace to those who repent increases to match it.

We might then conclude that because of God's grace it doesn't matter if we sin. In fact, the more we sin, the more grace we receive. More grace seems like a positive outcome.

Paul, however, thinks otherwise. He asks a rhetorical question: "Should we keep on sinning so that we showcase God's grace?"

He then answers his own question. "By no means!"

His emphatic response should remove any doubt from our minds that sinning to highlight God's grace is something to avoid.

To make sure we don't miss it, Paul circles back to this idea several verses later when he asks, "Shall we sin because we are not under the law but under grace?"

His response is again unequivocal. "By no means!"

We should celebrate God for the grace he gives us, but we should never intentionally do anything that would require him to give us more grace than he already has.

When it comes to persisting in sin, we must categorically say, "By no means!"

When have we sinned, thinking it didn't matter because God's grace would cover it? How can we do a better job of saying no to sin?

[Discover two other times when Paul says, "By no means!" in Romans 7:13 and Romans 11:1. Read a parallel passage in Romans 7:7.]

DAY 14: SLAVES

ROMANS 6:15–23

Don't you know that when you offer yourselves to someone as obedient slaves, you are slaves of the one you obey? (Romans 6:16)

We know the law reveals our sinful nature. We also know that when we follow Jesus, his grace covers our sins. Does this mean that because of Jesus we can keep on sinning? Of course not. That's foolish talk —and most dangerous thinking, because we become slaves to whatever we obey.

If we follow our sinful nature, we become slaves to sin. Sin leads to death. This is precisely what God told Adam would happen if he disobeyed. That he would die, and he did. So did Eve. With two notable exceptions—Enoch and Elijah—so did everyone who came after him. Death is a consequence of sin.

Yet, we can alternately choose to obey God. In this way, we become slaves of righteousness. This obedience, however, isn't to the law. Instead, it's obedience to Jesus's call to follow him. When we say yes to Jesus, we say no to our past life of sin.

This doesn't mean we won't sin anymore. We will. But as we follow Jesus—as we obey him—we rewire our thinking. Our hearts draw us to the pattern of his teaching. We give our allegiance to Jesus and what he says. When we do, he sets us free from being slaves to sin. Instead, we are now free to become slaves to righteousness.

Yet we don't need to live a righteous life to earn our salvation. Instead, we realize our right standing through the grace that only God can give.

This means we live a righteous life in *response* to our salvation only after we receive it. It's our way of saying thank you to Jesus for what he did for us when he died as the ultimate sacrifice to save us from the penalty our sins warrant.

Let's contrast these two types of slavery: being a slave to sin versus being a slave to righteousness.

The law, which reveals sin, causes us to be slaves to impurity. Another word for impurity is immorality. Sexual immorality may be what we first think of, but there are other forms of immorality as well. These include lying, stealing, assault, murder, corruption, and so forth. This impurity leads to increasing wickedness, which results in death.

Contrast this to our relationship with Jesus. Because of him, we are no longer slaves to sin. Instead, we become slaves to righteousness. Righteousness leads to holiness. Holiness results in eternal life.

Paul ends with a reminder that the wages of sin is death, but God's gift to us is eternal life through Jesus.

Are we more slaves to sin or slaves to righteousness? More directly, is our lifestyle moving us closer to death or closer to eternal life? If we don't like our answers to these two questions, what should our response be?

[Discover the two people who didn't die and went straight to be with God in Genesis 5:24 and 2 Kings 2:11.]

DAY 15: DEAD TO THE LAW
ROMANS 7:1–6

So, my brothers and sisters, you also died to the law through the body of Christ, that you might belong to another, to him who was raised from the dead, in order that we might bear fruit for God. (Romans 7:4)

Paul has an important lesson to teach us, and he wants to make sure we understand it. To help us grasp an otherwise abstract concept, he opens with an analogy we easily comprehend. It's about marriage. (Paul's example relates to the wife. Since wives often outlive their husbands, it's the more common scenario. But the concept applies to husbands too.)

When two people get married, they pledge

themselves to each other—and no one else. If one spouse cheats on the other, it's adultery. The law clearly says so. Through their marital vows, as supported by the law, the couple is bound to each other for as long as they live.

Yet when one dies, the law no longer applies. It would, after all, make no sense to require the surviving spouse to be faithful to someone who is no longer alive. Therefore, the death of one spouse negates the marriage covenant. The surviving spouse is free to marry another without penalty or reprisal.

When we say yes to Jesus, we align with his death, burial, and resurrection (Day 13). Our dying with him breaks the shackles of the law on us. It no longer applies. Just as the death of a spouse releases us from the requirements of marriage, our death with Jesus releases us from the requirements of the law.

Through Jesus, the law no longer holds us. It no longer demands that we comply with its legal constraints. We now belong to our Savior. We are to be faithful to him, and the law no longer applies. Instead of being bound to the law, we are now released from it so that we might bear fruit for God.

It's important to realize that we're not merely

free from the law. Instead, we're free from the law to bear fruit. This is a critical distinction.

Jesus teaches that he is the vine, and the Father is the gardener (John 15:1–17). The gardener will cut off every branch that bears no fruit. Therefore, if we bear no fruit for the Father, we risk being cut off from Jesus.

Yet, even if we bear fruit—which we should— we can expect the gardener to prune us. This pruning allows us to produce even more.

As long as we stay connected to Jesus, we will bear much fruit. He says so. Without him, we'll accomplish nothing.

As servants of Jesus, what is our view of the law? Are we staying connected to Jesus and him alone? What kind of fruit are we bearing for God?

[Discover more about bearing fruit for God in Luke 6:43 and Colossians 1:3–13.]

DAY 16: DELIVERANCE
THROUGH JESUS
ROMANS 7:7–25

Thanks be to God, who delivers me through Jesus Christ our Lord! So then, I myself in my mind am a slave to God's law, but in my sinful nature a slave to the law of sin. (Romans 7:25)

Paul just gave us a powerful teaching about the law and our relationship to it, which we covered in Day 15. Yet the clear principle doesn't always flow smoothly into practice. In fact, it's a bit bumpy.

The intent of the law was to teach God's people the right way to live. In doing so, it would move them toward righteousness. Aside from the reality that the law presented an impossible standard to follow, the law also revealed sin (Day 7). Because of the law, the people now knew what sin was in clear and concise detail.

Does that make the law sinful? Of course not. The law is holy, righteous, and good. This is God's law. Yet when we give in to our sinful nature, it makes us slaves to the law of sin. The result is two ways to look at the law: God's law and the law of sin.

Dealing with this is a challenge for Paul, just as it is for all of us.

Paul shares his agonizing struggle with this from personal experience. As if to emphasize his despair, he repeats the same idea several times, which he restates in various ways. A succinct summary is that he too often fails to do what he knows he should do. Instead, he ends up doing what he knows he shouldn't.

We can certainly identify with this struggle in our daily lives.

We strive to do what is right—and may even succeed most of the time—yet we sometimes fall short and don't do what is right. And we fail to do what we know we should do.

Other times, it's just the opposite. We know what we shouldn't do—and may even avoid it most of the time—yet we sometimes give in and do the wrong thing anyway. We fail and do what we shouldn't do.

It's quite a quandary. We may identify with Paul's deep despair when he says, "What a wretched man I am!"

What should our response be? Should we just give up and stop trying?

Of course not.

We have Jesus on our side. He has already rescued us. Through him we are delivered.

What should our response be when we don't do what we know we should do? What about when we do the things we know we shouldn't? How well do we do at thanking God for delivering us from this through Jesus?

[Discover more about God's law in Romans 8:7 and 1 Corinthians 9:21.]

DAY 17: THE SPIRIT IS LIFE
ROMANS 8:1–17

The mind governed by the flesh is death, but the mind governed by the Spirit is life and peace. (Romans 8:6)

Today's passage in Paul's letter opens with this succinct summary of the prior text (Day 16). If we identify with Paul's struggle to do what is right and not do what is wrong, the teacher's words provide us with much comfort. He simply says that through Jesus there's no condemnation. None. How reassuring.

This is because through Jesus we have the Holy Spirit within us. The law of the Spirit has set us free from the law of death.

Paul mentions Spirit—that's Spirit with a

capital S, as in the Holy Spirit—twenty-two times in this chapter, with sixteen times in today's passage alone.

Our focus verse serves as a smart capstone of Paul's teaching in this portion of his letter. If we let the flesh—that is, our sinful desires—govern our minds, the result is death. In contrast, if we let the Spirit—that is, the Holy Spirit Jesus sent us—govern our minds, the result is life and peace.

May the Holy Spirit govern our minds. Then we will receive life and experience peace.

Paul gives several contrasts between living by the flesh and living by the Holy Spirit.

Those who live by the flesh set their minds on what the flesh desires, that is, on carnal things. Yet if we live by the Spirit, we set our minds on what the Spirit desires, that is, on spiritual things.

If our flesh controls us, we are hostile to God. We don't submit to his law; we can't even do so. When we live by the flesh, it's impossible to please God. This is not the case when the Spirit controls us.

If we live by the flesh, we will die. But if we live by the Spirit, we put to death the sins of our body, and we will live.

When we align ourselves with Jesus—as his

follower, as his disciple, as his servant—the Holy Spirit lives within us. If we don't have the Holy Spirit, that means we don't belong to Jesus.

If we are to be led by the Holy Spirit, and realize his work in our lives, it starts with Jesus. Our future—both in this world and the next—begins when we follow Jesus.

Does our flesh or the Holy Spirit govern our minds? Are we experiencing the life and the peace that only Jesus's Spirit can provide? How can we more fully realize the Spirit at work within us?

[Discover more about the Holy Spirit in Luke 11:13, Luke 12:11–12, John 14:26, and Romans 8:26.]

BONUS CONTENT: GOD'S CHILDREN

The Spirit you received brought about your adoption to sonship. (Romans 8:15)

W hen we follow Jesus and become his disciples, Jesus's Spirit—the Holy Spirit—comes to live within us. The result is our adoption into God's family.

In this way, Jesus's Father becomes our Father—our Heavenly Father. God then calls us his children, and we call him Abba, Father.

Paul repeats a similar thought in another letter. He says that Jesus redeemed us and we are adopted (Galatians 4:4–6).

Regardless of our earthly families—whether

exemplary, not so good, or nonexistent—we can find assurance knowing we're also part of a spiritual family, which is faultless. God is our Father, and we are his children.

God is the ideal parent. He loves us completely and never makes mistakes in raising us. He disciplines us appropriately, as well as piling his grace and mercy on us. From a spiritual perspective, it's the perfect family. And it's our eternal family too.

Whatever we may think of our earthly family, it will one day end. But our spiritual family with Father God, Jesus his Son, and the Holy Spirit will last through all eternity.

This is what it means to be a child of God.

What do we think about God adopting us into his family? How well do we do in viewing him as our Heavenly Father?

[Discover more about being children of God in Galatians 3:26–27 and Philippians 2:14–15.]

DAY 18: ALL THINGS
ROMANS 8:18–30

We know that in all things God works for the good of those who love him, who have been called according to his purpose.
(Romans 8:28)

Today's focus verse is a favorite among many of Jesus's followers. It offers them comfort and provides encouragement amid the struggles we face. Yet, it's important to embrace the complete text.

Many shorten this sentiment to say that God works all things out for our good. But that succinct rendering skips two essential requirements.

The first is that it applies only to those who love God.

If we don't love God—Father, Son, and Holy Spirit—this promise doesn't apply to us. This love of God isn't an emotion or a feeling. It's an attitude that results in action.

We show our love to God in what we do for him, for his kingdom and his glory. Furthermore, we must love him above all others, with all our heart, soul, and mind. This is the greatest commandment (Matthew 22:36–40).

Second, it only applies to those who have been called according to his purpose.

At its basic level, God calls us to follow Jesus and live a life worthy of him. This means that loving God alone isn't enough. Yes, it's a great start, but remember that Jesus is the way to the Father; Jesus is not the destination (John 14:6).

When we are called to follow Jesus, it isn't merely for our benefit. It's to do so according to God's purpose. We shouldn't just take a onetime step toward Jesus and expect to continue living our lives as usual. This falls short of God's purpose for us.

Beyond our initial call to follow Jesus, God will call us to other things as well. We need to answer these calls and do what he wants us to do. This also is according to his purpose.

Therefore, a better recap of this verse is that when we love God and follow Jesus in obedience to what he says, our Lord will work all things out for our good.

Yet, there's more. God foreknew who would do this. He predestined them to conform to Jesus. They are called, justified, and glorified. But instead of viewing this as a succession of steps, we may be better off considering them as happening simultaneously. When we follow Jesus, we're foreknown by God, predestined, called, justified, and glorified.

With this as our framework, God will work out all things for our overall good.

Do we oversimplify this verse, like many others have? How do we show our love to God? In addition to following Jesus, what else is God calling us to do?

[Discover more about being called in 1 Corinthians 1:1, 1 Corinthians 1:9, Ephesians 1:18, 2 Thessalonians 2:14, 2 Timothy 1:9, and 1 Peter 5:10.]

DAY 19: NOTHING CAN SEPARATE US
ROMANS 8:31–39

Who shall separate us from the love of Christ? Shall trouble or hardship or persecution or famine or nakedness or danger or sword? (Romans 8:35)

Paul asks if anyone can separate us from Jesus's love. This may be a rhetorical question, but even if it isn't, we know that nothing can separate us from Jesus's love. He did, after all, come to Earth to die in our place as the ultimate sin sacrifice for all the wrong things we have done—and will ever do.

That's the epitome of love. Therefore, no one will ever be able to come between us and his love for us.

People can cause us great trouble. They can attack us, torment us, verbally assault us. Through it all, Jesus loves us.

We can endure hardship brought about by others. They can take what is ours. They can repress us. And they can abandon us when we're in need. Jesus never will. His love for us will continue through it all.

Next is persecution. When we follow Jesus, people may persecute us for our faith and how we put our faith into action. This goes beyond facing trouble or enduring hardship. Though the persecution could be verbal, it could also be physical. Jesus stands with us through it all. His love never wavers.

Consider famine. When we're hungry and lack the food we need, Jesus loves us amid our suffering.

If we're naked or need clothes to cover us, Jesus is there with us.

If we face danger, Jesus stands by us.

If our life is threatened, Jesus remains with us. And even if our life is taken, we will spend eternity with our Savior.

Through all these things, we can overcome them through Jesus and his love for us.

Yet Paul has more to share.

Neither death nor life will separate us from Jesus's love.

Angels can't interrupt Jesus's love, and demons are powerless to oppose it.

Nothing in our present reality and nothing in our future will separate us from Jesus.

Neither will any power come between us and Jesus's love. This includes both those with worldly power and those with supernatural power.

Last, we know that some people are afraid of heights, and others fear depths, either in the water or underground. Yet in both situations, Jesus's love is there with us.

In fact, nothing in all of creation will ever be able to separate us from God's great love for us that is manifest in Jesus our Lord.

Which items on this list do we struggle with the most to accept? Knowing that nothing can separate us from Jesus's love, is there anything that we should fear? What should our response be to Jesus's love?

[Discover more about Jesus's love for us in 2 Thessalonians 2:16–17 and 1 John 3:16.]

DAY 20: THE POTTER'S WILL

ROMANS 9:1–21

Does not the potter have the right to make out of the same lump of clay some pottery for special purposes and some for common use? (Romans 9:21)

An interesting word picture that helps us better understand God and our relationship to him is the potter and the clay. He is the Potter, and we are his clay. Given that God is our Creator, it's fitting to see him as an artist who molds clay into various objects, according to his will and aligned with his preference.

Some people might claim it's unfair for God to make us into whoever—or whatever—he wants us to be. But are we able to resist what he wants to do?

Of course not. Who are we, as his creation, to question our Creator? (Romans 9:20, quoting Isaiah 29:16). It would be arrogant for us to confront him and his will for us.

We mustn't forget that he is our Lord, and we are his creation. May he create us to be whatever he desires. May we accept what he does—in faith that it is what is best for us (Day 18).

Extending this metaphor of potter and clay further, we see that not all clay is moldable. Some clay is unusable in its present condition.

If clay is too dry, a potter can't form it into anything. It's useless. So the potter mixes water into the clay and seals it in a bag. He sets the bag of clay aside and allows it to sit. This gives time for the moisture to permeate the clay and make it moldable.

The other extreme is clay that is too wet. If the potter tried to make something out of it, it wouldn't hold its shape. It would collapse into a useless blob. In this instance, the potter needs to dry out the clay before he can use it. He needs to remove the excess water from it. To do this, he sets it aside, uncovered, so that the surrounding air may remove moisture from it.

Clay that is too dry and clay that is too wet is

useless to the potter. He can't make anything with it. He must set it aside and wait until it becomes usable.

In this way, we see that we have a role in how the Potter uses us. If we allow him to make us into whoever he wants us to be, he happily forms us according to his will. Yet if we resist becoming what he wants us to be, he sets us aside until we're ready.

May we be the type of clay that's moldable and not the type that resists our Potter's will.

What kind of clay are we? If we feel God has set us aside, is it because we're resisting what he wants to do in our lives? How can we better accept what God is making us into?

[Discover more about the potter and the clay in Isaiah 64:8, Jeremiah 18:1–6, and Lamentations 4:2.]

BONUS CONTENT: FOR
THE SAKE OF OTHERS

For I could wish that I myself were cursed and cut off from Christ for the sake of my people, those of my own race, the people of Israel. (Romans 9:3–4)

I t's easy to say we love others. It's harder to show it, to prove our words through action. Despite what I may profess, I fear I may be more selfish than I care to admit. I may not love those closest to me as fully as I think I do. And to be honest, I may not love those who are not so close that much at all.

Jesus, however, shows his love for us—and for everyone—by dying in our place. We mess up; we deserve punishment. In fact, our mistakes are so many that our sentence is death.

Out of his deep love for us, Jesus volunteers to take our place and receive our punishment. He dies so we don't have to. This is the ultimate expression of true love.

Yes, there are some I would die for. But not everyone. My love has limits. God's love does not. Jesus proves that.

Yet, as incredible as it seems, Paul offers to take love one step farther. His love for his people is so deep, his compassion so strong, that he's willing to be separated forever from Jesus if it will save them, the Jewish people. Not some of them, but all of them, even those who are trying to kill him and want him dead.

Paul claims he's willing to spend eternity in hell, forever separated from Jesus, so that his people can spend eternity in heaven, forever in community with Jesus.

He offers to give up so much. Frankly, I wonder if he really means it. Or maybe it's just hyperbole, an exaggeration to make his point. Of course, he can't really carry out such a grand offer, such an extravagant show of love.

Yet this certainly gives us something to consider,

showing love profoundly like Jesus and professing it deeply like Paul.

How do we best show our love to others, both those closest to us and those who are not? How concerned are we for people who don't yet know Jesus? What are we doing to bring them to him?

[Discover more about dying for another in John 15:13 and Romans 5:7. Read what Caiaphas says about Jesus dying for us in John 11:49–52.]

DAY 21: FAITH VERSUS LAW
ROMANS 9:22–33

The Gentiles, who did not pursue righteousness, have obtained it, a righteousness that is by faith. (Romans 9:30)

In today's passage, Paul acknowledges a truth that would shock many of his own people, even though they should know better—for the Old Testament Scripture foretold it. He says it was God's plan to call both the Jews and the Gentiles for glory. Then he quotes some prophets to back up his claim.

Hosea says God will call them my people, even though they aren't. He will love them, even though they aren't his chosen ones (Hosea 2:23). He'll call them children of the living God (Hosea 1:10).

Isaiah says that only some of the Hebrew people will be saved (Isaiah 10:22–23). Only some of them will survive (Isaiah 1:9).

As we've covered, God gave his people the law to teach them the right way to live (Day 16). By following it, they would become righteous. Yet it was an impossible standard to meet. What the law accomplished, however, was that it revealed sin and the need for a better solution (Day 7). The partial solution was an annual animal sin sacrifice to atone temporarily for the people's sins, but it needed to be repeated each year for centuries.

Jesus came to earth to provide a total and permanent solution. It didn't involve following the law to earn salvation. Instead, it involved accepting Jesus through faith.

Therefore, the Gentiles, who didn't try to be righteous by following the law, obtained their righteousness anyway. It's a righteousness they received through faith when they followed Jesus.

Conversely, the Jewish people who pursued the law as their path to righteousness fell short and missed out. Yet not all did. Some Hebrew people received their salvation. But this wasn't through following the law alone; it was through faith.

Abraham is an example of this (Romans 4:13–

17). We covered him in Day 9. Yet Abraham isn't the only Old Testament character noted for his faith. Hebrews 11 highlights the faith of many more: Abel, Enoch, Noah, Isaac, Jacob, Sarah, Joseph, Moses's parents, Moses, and Rahab. There are also Gideon, Barak, Samson, Jephthah, David, and Samuel.

God wants all people to be saved (1 Timothy 2:3–5). For the Jewish people, this starts with pursuing righteousness through the law and culminates with faith. The Gentile people, who don't follow the law, receive their righteousness by faith alone.

We are all—both Jew and Gentile—saved by faith (Romans 10:10 and Ephesians 2:8–9). Our faith is what matters to God.

How can the faith of these Old Testament characters encourage us today? How should we view the law? How can we balance right living (righteousness) with faith?

[Discover more about faith in Matthew 8:5–11, Matthew 9:22, Mark 2:5, and Acts 14:8–10.]

DAY 22: THE LAW
CULMINATES IN JESUS
ROMANS 10:1–13

Christ is the culmination of the law so that there may be righteousness for everyone who believes. (Romans 10:4)

P aul opens today's passage sharing the desire of his heart and his steadfast prayer. He yearns for the Israelites to be saved. This shouldn't surprise us because he already asserted he's willing to be forever damned if it would save his people. (See Bonus Content: For the Sake of Others.)

He acknowledges that his people are zealous for God. Unfortunately, being zealous isn't enough, because their zeal doesn't stem from knowledge. It's based on works. They're zealous in following the

Old Testament law. They're most conscientious in adhering to the letter of the law to the very best of their ability. Yet it isn't enough.

Jesus is the answer they seek—the answer they need. He is the culmination of the law. Everyone who believes in him will be found righteous in God's eyes. They will live by faith and not by following a law that prescribes righteous acts.

He then says exactly what to do.

We need to proclaim Jesus as Lord—as the Lord of our life and all we do. Then we must believe wholeheartedly that God raised him from the dead. This is what it takes to be saved (Romans 10:9).

That's all there is to it. At least that's all there is to starting down the path on our journey with Jesus. We'll now spend the rest of our lives building upon this initial foundation of faith.

Next, Paul reframes the concept to make sure we don't miss it. It's with our hearts that we believe and are justified. It's with our words that we profess our faith. This is salvation (Romans 10:10).

To support his assertion, Paul paraphrases Isaiah 28:16: Anyone who believes in Jesus will never regret it. This applies to both God's chosen people—the Jews—and everyone else, which would be the Gentiles. Our background doesn't matter.

Our heritage doesn't matter. And our rules don't matter. Believing in Jesus is what counts. In fact, it's the only thing that matters.

Paul wraps up this passage with a succinct summary of his teaching, of this essential instruction about salvation. He says that every person who calls on Jesus will be saved (Romans 10:13).

This is how the Old Testament law culminates in Jesus. That means the law reaches its climax and ends with Jesus. There is no greater conclusion. There is no other way to be saved.

How should we embrace Jesus as the culmination of the law? Does what we've heard about salvation differ from what Paul says in today's passage? What can we learn from Paul's teaching that there's no difference between Jew and Gentile?

[Discover the culmination of the ages in 1 Corinthians 10:11 and Hebrews 9:26.]

Have you declared Jesus as your Lord and believe he rose from the dead? If not, I urge for you to do so today.

DAY 23: PREACH THE WORD

ROMANS 10:14–21

How, then, can they call on the one they have not believed in?
And how can they believe in the one of whom they have not
heard? And how can they hear without someone preaching to
them? And how can anyone preach unless they are sent?
(Romans 10:14–15)

Paul has just written that everyone who calls on Jesus will be saved. That's simple enough. But underneath this simple instruction lay a series of prerequisites. These requirements, however, don't apply to the person calling on Jesus. It applies to what happens before-hand, to how they get to that point.

How can people call on Jesus if they haven't yet

believed in him? In order to believe in him, however, they must first hear about him. But to hear about Jesus, someone needs to tell them. And how can that person preach the good news of Jesus unless they are sent to do so?

This seems to highlight the essential need for missionaries (and ministers) to tell others about Jesus. Yet this is only one plausible conclusion. Yes, we need missionaries. But not everyone can do that —at least not in the conventional sense.

Missionaries also need support. This is where the rest of us come in. This includes financial support, emotional support, and especially prayer support. Everyone can do that. Everyone should. This suggests we can either go to tell others the good news of Jesus or support those who do. But being a missionary for Jesus or supporting missionaries for Jesus aren't the only two solutions.

We can do more. We should be prepared to do more.

It's important for all of us to tell others about Jesus too. If we don't, who will? Maybe someone else will, or maybe no one will. If no one else tells them about Jesus, then their one chance was with us. May we not miss that chance. May we make the most of every opportunity.

God can send us out to preach Jesus to the masses. This can be in person or through various forms of media.

Yet God can also send us out to preach Jesus to just one person. This one-to-one approach is exactly what God did with Ananias to guide Paul (Acts 9:10–18). The Lord later told Philip to drop what he was doing to help the Ethiopian treasurer (Acts 8:26–40).

Regardless of what God asks us to do in telling others about him, may our answer be yes.

If we aren't a missionary for Jesus, how can we support those who are? Who is God urging us to tell about Jesus? Have we obeyed, or are we trying to talk ourselves out of it?

[Discover more about being prepared in Matthew 25:1–13, 2 Timothy 4:2, and 1 Peter 3:15–16.]

DAY 24: NOT REJECTED
ROMANS 11:1–10

God did not reject his people, whom he foreknew. (Romans 11:2)

Some Christians think the Gentiles who follow Jesus have replaced the Jews as God's chosen people. They assume this means all the promises God made in the Old Testament to the Hebrew people no longer apply to them and have been transferred to Jesus's New Testament church.

Paul's teaching in his letter to the Romans doesn't support that assertion at all. God has not rejected his chosen people. Paul says so directly in today's focus verse. And we'll address the subject more in our studies for Days 25 and 26.

To show how absurd this is, Paul reminds us that he is a Jew, a descendant of Abraham from the tribe of Benjamin. Not only did Paul write about half the books of the New Testament, but all the New Testament writers (except for Luke) were Jewish. If these Jewish writers had been rejected, we wouldn't have the New Testament to read today.

God did not reject his people. He foreknew them.

Paul's second proof that God did not reject his people comes from the prophet Elijah. He's coming off a great spiritual victory, yet he's discouraged. He thinks he's the only one left who follows God. And his enemies—particularly Queen Jezebel—want to kill him.

The Lord is quick to correct Elijah. He is not the only one left. There are seven thousand others who have remained faithful (1 Kings 19:1–18).

This reminds me of a personal experience. One Sunday, the Holy Spirit prompted me to pray for a friend's daughter. She was about to start her junior year of high school. She sat in front of me at church with her best friend.

They were most receptive when I said I wanted

to pray for them and the upcoming school year. But they were also somber. One told me they were the only two Christians in the entire high school. The other nodded her sad agreement.

I knew that wasn't correct. Many students in the school of over one thousand, as well as a lot of teachers, were followers of Jesus. It's just that these two girls didn't know them. They were sure they were alone. Part of my prayer for them—which they received expectantly—was that God would show them other believers in their school.

In this way, I saw a modern-day example of Elijah's despondency played out in real life. Just as Elijah was not alone in his faith, neither were these two girls.

With Paul having twice confirmed that God foreknew his chosen people, we see that God has not rejected them. Even at the time of Paul writing his letter to the Romans, a remnant of God's chosen people have been chosen by grace. They aren't working to earn their salvation by following the law. Instead, they receive their salvation by the grace of God.

It matters not whether we're Jew or Gentile; God's grace saves us. God foreknew this.

What should we do when we think we're the only believer at school, work, or in the neighborhood? How can we find other believers to stand with? How can we find comfort in knowing that God foreknew us?

[Discover more about those God foreknew in Romans 8:29.]

DAY 25: GRAFTED BACK

ROMANS 11:11–24

If they do not persist in unbelief, they will be grafted in, for God is able to graft them in again. (Romans 11:23)

W hen a branch from one tree is grafted onto another tree—that is, connected to it—the grafted branch receives nourishment from the roots of the tree it's attached to. In this way, a branch originally from a tree with weak roots can be supported by the foundation of a tree with good stock.

So it is when God grafts our branches onto his tree. This is the background for today's passage.

The Jewish people are branches of God's tree, a cultivated olive tree. The Gentiles—all the rest of us

—are like wild olive branches. Because of their persistent unbelief, God has cut off many of the Jewish branches. In their place, he's grafted us—as wild olive branches—onto the tree, that is, onto him. We're now connected to God's cultivated tree and receive nourishing sap from it.

This fact may make us falsely proud that we have been grafted in because of our supposed superior status, while many Jewish people have been cut off. We shouldn't be arrogant, however, about our right standing with the Father. Instead, we should quake with concern, knowing that just as he removed some of his chosen people from his tree, he can likewise remove us if we fall back into unbelief.

Yet, we must realize that the Jewish branches can still recover. God can—and will—graft them back onto his tree in the same way he grafted us, the wild olive branches. All that his chosen people (the Jews) need to do is believe in him, just as the Gentiles did. Adhering to the law will not save Jewish people; their faith will (Day 21).

Both Jew and Gentile alike—the natural branches and the wild ones—are made holy because we're connected to holy roots. As the roots are, so are the branches attached to them. This includes the original branches, as well as the ones—both wild and natural—grafted onto God's tree.

How should we consider ourselves to be a wild olive branch grafted onto God's tree? Do we take unwarranted pride in being grafted in? Why should we tremble about our status as a grafted branch?

[Discover more about unbelief in Mark 9:24 and Hebrews 3:19.]

Do you want to help Jewish people get grafted in again? I do. One option is to support the work of Jews for Jesus (jewsforjesus.org). Will you join me?

DAY 26: A TEMPORARY HARDENING

ROMANS 11:25–32

*Israel has experienced a hardening in part until the full
number of the Gentiles has come in, and in this way all
Israel will be saved.* (Romans 11:25–26)

Though many of the Jewish people have
been pruned from God's cultivated tree,
not all have. Some remained connected
through faith (Day 21). Even more encouraging,
others can be re-grafted (Day 25).

Many of God's chosen people have experienced
a hardening, which has caused them to be cut from
God's holy tree. But this is not a permanent
removal; it's a temporary condition. The hardening
will last until the full number of Gentiles has been

grafted in. Then the Jewish people—the ones presently separated from God—will be re-grafted onto his tree. We can look forward to this with much anticipation. What a glorious day this will be.

Sometimes God hardens the people's hearts, and other times the people do it themselves.

When God hardens a person's heart, it accomplishes his purpose in the grand scope of his creation. Though the idea of God hardening people's hearts may seem unfair, remember that he is our Sovereign Creator and can do whatever he wants with what he made. He is the Potter, and we are the clay (Day 20). He forms us to do whatever purpose he desires for us to accomplish.

Consider the pharaoh when the people lived as slaves in Egypt as forced laborers. God, through Moses, sought to bring about the people's release. Many times, Pharaoh agreed but then changed his mind, because God repeatedly hardened his heart (Exodus 4:21 and several more times in Exodus chapters 7–14).

Why did God do this? One thought is that God was building up to a grand finale. When they left, the Egyptians viewed them favorably and gave them whatever they asked for. In this way, they plundered the land (Exodus 12:36).

Later, when Pharaoh chased them, Pharaoh and his army perished, while Israel was saved (Exodus 14:28). This protected the people from later being recaptured, driven back to Egypt, and forced to return to slavery.

Aside from God hardening people's hearts, other times people can harden their own. This is intentional and of their own volition. The result is they're unable to see God's goodness and understand his ways.

May we never harden our hearts toward God.

How should we best understand the idea of God hardening someone's heart? When have we hardened our hearts toward our Lord? What should we do to protect ourselves from this occurring in the future?

[Discover more about people who hardened their hearts in 2 Chronicles 36:13, Psalm 95:6–11, Ezekiel 3:7–8, Mark 8:17, and Hebrews 4:7.]

DAY 27: FROM, THROUGH, AND FOR HIM

ROMANS 11:33–36

For from him and through him and for him are all things. To him be the glory forever! Amen. (Romans 11:36)

Today's passage reads like a doxology—an expression of praise to God. We might take this as a sign that Paul is about to end his letter, but he is not. He has much more to say. Maybe he inserts an interlude of praise here merely as a pause until he transitions into the rest of his writing.

Paul opens his praise of God by proclaiming the deep riches of his Lord's wisdom. We're unable to understand God's decisions or comprehend how he works things together according to his will.

Paul follows this by asking three insightful questions. First, who can know what God is thinking? Second, who are we to offer advice to our Lord? Third, who has given anything to the Almighty that he must repay? The answer to all three is no one.

Then Paul proclaims that all things come from God, through God, and for God. Let's explore this.

To begin, we know all things are from God. He is our Creator. The Father, Holy Spirit, and Son all take part in creating us and our world (Genesis 1:2 and John 1:2–3). When God says, let us make man in our image, he's talking to himself: Father, Son, and Holy Spirit (Genesis 1:26).

God is our Creator, and we are the created. We —along with the world we live in—all come from him. May we never forget this.

Next, we know all things are through him. God's creation established the foundation for life. He designed trees to produce seeds that grow more trees. He designed animals that produce offspring. And he designed people to procreate. Every living thing today comes from what he created those many years ago. In this way, all things are through him.

Even more so, we are through him spiritually as

well. Our salvation—our eternal life—comes through Jesus. Though our wrong behavior deserves the death penalty, Jesus dies in our place as the perfect sacrifice to satisfy God's judgment against us. Jesus offers us the grace and mercy we don't deserve to counter the judgment we do deserve. In this way, all things are through him.

Last, we know all things are for him. Why did God create people? To be in community with him. In the beginning, God walks in the garden of Eden to be with his creation (Genesis 3:8). At the end of time, we will be with him in the new heaven and new earth (Revelation 21:1–3). Between these two bookend events of the Bible, we have the potential to be with God as well. Though this is an imperfect reflection of what was and what will be, we can be in community with him now (1 Thessalonians 5:10).

Beyond this, we must live for God (Acts 17:28 and 2 Corinthians 5:15). We also serve him (Luke 4:8 and 1 Peter 4:11). In this way, we do all things for him.

All things are from God, through him, and for him. We give him the glory forever. Amen.

How can we best thank God for creating us and our world?
How can we acknowledge that all things come from him?
How can we best live our lives for our Lord?

[Discover more about giving God glory forever in Psalm 72:19, 2 Peter 3:18, and Jude 1:25.]

BONUS CONTENT: ROMANS
REFERENCES THE OLD TESTAMENT

"Who has ever given to God, that God should repay them?"
(Romans 11:35)

The book of Romans contains fifty-six verses that make seventy-four Old Testament references, more than any other book of the Bible. Even the scripturally deep book of Hebrews, which comes in second, only has forty-two.

The result is a rich teaching that connects followers of Jesus with his Old Testament heritage —one that we receive through him.

Here's a list of the verses in Romans that spring from the Jewish Scriptures:

- Romans 1:17 references Habakkuk 2:4
- Romans 2:6 quotes from Psalm 62:12 and Proverbs 24:12
- Romans 2:24 draws from Isaiah 52:5 and Ezekiel 36:20, 22
- Romans 3:4 quotes from Psalm 51:4
- Romans 3:12 quotes from Psalm 14:1–3, Psalm 53:1–3, and Ecclesiastes 7:20
- Romans 3:13 quotes Psalm 5:9 and Psalm 140:3
- Romans 3:14 references Psalm 10:7
- Romans 3:17 quotes Isaiah 59:8
- Romans 3:18 quotes Psalm 36:1
- Romans 4:3 quotes Genesis 15:6
- Romans 4:8 quotes Psalm 32:1–2
- Romans 4:17 quotes Genesis 17:5
- Romans 4:18 quotes Genesis 15:5
- Romans 4:22 quotes Genesis 15:6
- Romans 7:7 quotes Exodus 20:17 and Deuteronomy 5:21
- Romans 8:36 quotes Psalm 44:22
- Romans 9:7 quotes Genesis 21:12
- Romans 9:9 quotes Genesis 18:10 and Genesis 18:14
- Romans 9:12 quotes Genesis 25:23
- Romans 9:13 quotes Malachi 1:2–3

- Romans 9:15 quotes Exodus 33:19
- Romans 9:17 quotes Exodus 9:16
- Romans 9:20 draws from Isaiah 29:16 and Isaiah 45:9
- Romans 9:25 quotes Hosea 2:23
- Romans 9:26 quotes Hosea 1:10
- Romans 9:28 references Isaiah 10:22–23
- Romans 9:29 quotes Isaiah 1:9
- Romans 9:33 references Isaiah 8:14 and quotes Isaiah 28:16
- Romans 10:5 quotes Leviticus 18:5
- Romans 10:6 quotes Deuteronomy 30:12
- Romans 10:7 alludes to Deuteronomy 30:13
- Romans 10:8 quotes Deuteronomy 30:14
- Romans 10:11 references Isaiah 28:16
- Romans 10:13 quotes Joel 2:32
- Romans 10:15 quotes Isaiah 52:7
- Romans 10:16 quotes Isaiah 53:1
- Romans 10:18 quotes Psalm 19:4
- Romans 10:19 quotes Deuteronomy 32:21
- Romans 10:20 quotes Isaiah 65:1
- Romans 10:21 quotes Isaiah 65:2

- Romans 11:3 quotes 1 Kings 19:10 and 1 Kings 19:14
- Romans 11:4 quotes 1 Kings 19:18
- Romans 11:8 draws from Deuteronomy 29:4 and Isaiah 29:10
- Romans 11:10 quotes Psalm 69:22–23
- Romans 11:27 draws from Isaiah 27:9, Isaiah 59:20–21, and Jeremiah 31:33–34
- Romans 11:34 quotes Isaiah 40:13
- Romans 11:35 quotes Job 41:11
- Romans 12:19 quotes Deuteronomy 32:35
- Romans 12:20 quotes Proverbs 25:21–22
- Romans 13:9 quotes Exodus 20:13–15, 17, Deuteronomy 5:17–19, 21, and Leviticus 19:18
- Romans 14:11 quotes Isaiah 45:23
- Romans 15:3 quotes Psalm 69:9
- Romans 15:9 quotes 2 Samuel 22:50 and Psalm 18:49
- Romans 15:10 draws from Deuteronomy 32:43
- Romans 15:11 quotes Psalm 117:1
- Romans 15:12 references Isaiah 11:10
- Romans 15:21 quotes Isaiah 52:15

Why do you think Paul included so many Old Testament references in his letter? What can we learn from them?

[Discover more about the importance of Scripture in Deuteronomy 11:19, Psalm 119:11, and 2 Timothy 3:16.]

DAY 28: LIVING SACRIFICES
ROMANS 12:1–2

Therefore . . . offer your bodies as a living sacrifice, holy and pleasing to God—this is your true and proper worship.
(Romans 12:1)

C hapter 12 of Romans opens with the pivotal word *therefore*. Looking at yesterday's study, we see that all things are from God, through God, and for God. We give him the glory (Day 27).

Therefore, because of this, Paul urges us to offer our bodies as a living sacrifice. Doing so is holy; it pleases God. It serves as true worship; it's proper adoration. It's our response to him for who he is and what he has done and is doing for us.

When we think of the word *sacrifice*, our minds take us to death. All Old Testament sacrifices resulted in the death of an animal. This was as God prescribed in the law.

In the New Testament, Jesus offers himself as a sacrifice, dying on the cross in our place to make good all the wrong that we've done. Jesus's death isn't the end. It paves the way for his resurrection. A resurrection isn't the normal outcome of a sacrificial death.

But Paul isn't telling us to sacrifice ourselves through our deaths. He's telling us to sacrifice ourselves through our lives. That is, to let our lives be a living sacrifice to our Lord. Doing so is holy; it pleases God. It emerges as true and proper worship.

Though we often think of singing praises to God as worship (and rightly so), what if we reframe our thinking to embrace how we live our lives as worship? In this way, everything we do throughout our day can serve as our true and proper worship.

Paul provides two suggestions for how to do this, how to offer ourselves as living sacrifices.

First, he tells us not to do things as the rest of the world does. Just because everyone else does something, doesn't mean we should. In fact, there's a high likelihood that we shouldn't do what everyone else does. We're not to follow their example. They aren't a pattern for us to adhere to. Instead, we live our lives differently than the world. Our behavior should make us stand out in a God-honoring way.

Second, we're to transform our thinking. This means renewing our minds. We must reprogram our thoughts, not to align with the world's perspective, but to seek to follow God's. Jesus provides our best example of how to do this. Paul follows his example (1 Corinthians 11:1).

In addition to this, and as we covered yesterday, we must live for God (Acts 17:28 and 2 Corinthians 5:15). We also serve him (Luke 4:8 and 1 Peter 4:11).

If we reject what the world does, transform our thinking, live for God, and serve him, we are well on our way to being a living sacrifice.

How can we make our lives more like the living sacrifice Paul talks about? What actions of the world do we wrongly follow? What can we do to transform our thinking? How well do we do in seeing that everything we do serves as an act of worship?

[Discover more about living as a sacrifice in 1 Peter 2:4–10.]

DAY 29: ONE BODY
WITH MANY MEMBERS
ROMANS 12:3–8

In Christ we, though many, form one body, and each member belongs to all the others. (Romans 12:5)

Consider the various parts of our bodies. We have arms and legs, fingers and toes. We have eyes, ears, and a mouth. Last, we have internal organs that help us breathe and process food to give us energy. There are many other components of our body as well.

Some parts stand out, and we celebrate them. Other parts we choose to keep covered (and rightly so). And others exist inside our bodies, working unseen to keep us alive. We need each element if we are to be a complete person. Our arms can't tell our legs, "We don't need you," and still expect to move about. Our ears can't tell our eyes to "go away" and still be able to see.

When we follow Jesus, we collectively form one spiritual body. Each part belongs to the others. Each part is necessary for the whole body to function.

With each of us being gifted in different ways, some members of the body of Christ prophecy, others serve, and some teach. Other members encourage, give, lead, or show mercy.

Problems arise, however, when we don't want to do what God has graciously given us to do, instead wanting to do what someone else is doing. If we are to serve, perhaps we shouldn't try to teach. If God gifts us to be an encourager, we'd be wrong to push that gift aside and try to prophesy.

Moreover, we must not look down on those who have different functions in the body of Christ. All parts are needed to complete Jesus's body, to function as a complete unit in the manner he intended.

Some people apply this teaching of a body to a local church. Though there's merit in realizing that each person has a role to play in their congregation, this misapplies Paul's teaching that there is one body, as in the universal church. There aren't many bodies, with one at each local congregation. There's just one body, and it's worldwide.

In his final prayer before his execution, Jesus prays that we—his future followers—will be one, just as he and his Father are one. Why is this? By being unified as one, we become the optimum witness to the world so that they may believe (John 17:20–21).

Jesus wants us to be members of one body and not several diverse and contentious smaller bodies that don't get along. He wants us to be the universal body of Christ.

How well do we do at living as the body of Christ? What role do we play in the body? Are we content with that role? How can we best support the other parts of the body?

[Discover more about the body of Christ in 1 Corinthians 6:15, Ephesians 2:19–20, Ephesians 3:6, Ephesians 4:25, Ephesians 5:29–30, and Colossians 3:15.]

DAY 30: LOVE
ROMANS 12:9–21

Love must be sincere. Hate what is evil; cling to what is good.
(Romans 12:9)

Today's passage reminds us of the book of Proverbs, with many thought-provoking one-liners. Paul lists twenty-one concise instructions. Each one could have its own chapter. Instead, we'll list them all—along with supporting Scripture references—as a springboard for further contemplation.

1. **Love must be sincere**: We truly love others, just as Jesus loves us (Ephesians 5:25–27).

2. **Hate evil and embrace good**: Avoiding what is wrong, we focus on what is right (Luke 6:45).

3. **Be devoted to one another in love**: Peter says to love one another deeply, from our heart (1 Peter 1:22).

4. **Honor others as much as we honor ourselves**: Jesus gives us a parable that encourages humility (Luke 14:8–11).

5. **Serve God with zeal and spiritual fervor**: Serve God and only him (Luke 4:8 and Luke 16:13).

6. **Be joyful in hope**: Placing our hope in God, he fills us with joy and peace (Romans 15:13).

7. **Be patient in affliction**: When suffering, we stand firm until Jesus returns (James 5:7–8).

8. **Be faithful in prayer**: Like Paul, we continue praying for others (Colossians 1:9).

9. **Share with God's people in need**: Paul encouraged the church in Corinth to help the Jerusalem believers in need (1 Corinthians 16:1–3).

10. **Practice hospitality**: Show hospitality to strangers (Hebrews 13:2).

11. **Bless and do not curse those who persecute you**: We love our enemies and pray for our oppressors (Matthew 5:43–44).

12. **Rejoice with those who are happy**: We're glad and celebrate with others (Philippians 2:18).

13. **Mourn with those who are sad**: Jesus comforted Martha and Mary over the death of their brother (John 11:21–28).

14. **Live in harmony with one another**: We agree with others and don't cause division (1 Corinthians 1:10).

15. **Do not be proud, but be willing to associate with people of low position**: When we take a lowly position, we become great in God's eyes (Matthew 18:4).

16. **Don't be conceited**: We resist holding an unwarranted high opinion of ourselves, and instead we control our ego (Galatians 5:26).

17. **Do not repay anyone evil for evil**:
    The Old Testament told us, "an eye for
    an eye" (a command for moderation),
    but Jesus told us to go the extra mile
    (Matthew 5:38–42).

18. **Do what is right in the eyes of
    everyone**: Strive to do what is right
    before both God and people
    (2 Corinthians 8:21).

19. **Live at peace with everyone**: Make
    every effort to live peacefully with all
    people (Hebrews 12:14).

20. **Do not take revenge, but leave
    room for God's wrath**: Our Lord will
    avenge us when wronged (Deuteronomy
    32:35).

21. **Do not be overcome by evil, but
    overcome evil with good**: Turn from
    evil and do good (1 Peter 3:11).

*Which of these instructions do we need to do better at? What
should we do to make it happen? How can we thank God for
helping us in these areas?*

[Discover more about love in 1 Corinthians 13:4–6.]

DAY 31: SUBMIT TO
GOVERNING AUTHORITIES
ROMANS 13:1–7

Therefore, it is necessary to submit to the authorities, not only because of possible punishment but also as a matter of conscience. (Romans 13:5)

A s Paul continues his letter, he moves to the topic of governmental authorities. He says we should be subject to them. This is because God has established every governing authority.

This teaching gives me pause. Every authority? Surely, we can suggest some exceptions—some evil, malicious authorities who oppose us and our faith. Yet Paul doesn't provide for extenuating circumstances. God established them all, and we should be subject to them. Rebelling against the authorities God established rebels against what God instituted. The result will be judgment. This is hard to accept —at least for me.

Paul explains the logic behind his command. If we do what is right—that is, if we obey the law—we will have no reason to fear. God put them in authority to do good. They are his servants to punish wrongdoers. Therefore, it's necessary to submit to them. This is not only to avoid punishment but also because it's the right thing to do.

We may want to dismiss Paul's instruction as out of touch with today's reality, where many people live under government authority that's hostile to their faith, even to the point of imprisoning and killing them.

Yet Paul lived in the Roman Empire, which was hostile toward people of faith, especially those who aligned with Jesus.

Even though he was a Roman citizen, Paul— along with many of his associates—was often imprisoned. He was also punished repeatedly (2 Corinthians 11:23–25). History tells us that many who professed their faith in Jesus met a brutal death in the Colosseum. And like Jesus, others were executed. The situation in the Roman Empire then seems to match the situation facing many in our world today.

But when Paul tells us to submit to those in authority, he gives no qualifiers.

We do, however, have one exception, exemplified by Peter (Acts 5:17–29). When the religious leaders arrest the apostles and put them in jail, an angel releases them and tells them to continue telling others about Jesus. They do and get in trouble for it. Brought before the Sanhedrin—the religious council—the high priest reminds them he ordered them not to talk about Jesus.

Peter replies, "We must obey God and not you."

This seems to be the one exception to Paul's command to submit to authorities. If submitting to them violates what God tells us to do, we should follow God and not them. Yet in all other instances, we are not to oppose them.

Paul wraps up with some practical teaching of what to do. If we owe taxes, we must pay them. If we owe revenue, we must remit it. If we owe respect, we must respect. If we owe honor, we must offer it.

How well do we do at submitting to government authorities? Have we given them what we owe: taxes, revenue, respect, and honor? If we've fallen short, are we willing to repent of our error and correct it?

[Discover more about those in authority in 1 Timothy 2:1–2.]

DAY 32: LOVE MATTERS MOST
ROMANS 13:8–10

Love is the fulfillment of the law. (Romans 13:10)

The Old Testament law—as found in the books of Exodus, Leviticus, Numbers, and Deuteronomy—consists of numerous rules of what to do and what not to do to meet God's expectations. Bible scholars identify 613 such laws. That's a lot of rules. In addition, well-meaning adherents attempted to clarify them with exacting specificity, giving detailed examples of what to do and what to avoid. This amounted to tens of thousands of more religious expectations.

An expert in these religious laws comes to Jesus

with a question. "What's the greatest command-ment in all the law?"

Jesus says that we must love our Lord God with all our heart, soul, and mind. This is the first commandment, and it's also the greatest of them all.

But Jesus doesn't stop at one. He adds another. "The second greatest commandment is to love others as much as we love ourselves." These two commands smartly cover everything in the law and everything the prophets said.

This neatly reduces the 613 Old Testament laws, along with their expanded guidelines, down to two essential commands (Matthew 22:35–40).

If we love God and love others, we meet the law's requirements.

With this as our background, let's move back to where we wrapped up yesterday. When Paul told us we're to give our government what we owe them—be it taxes, revenue, respect, or honor—it fell under the general command to give to everyone what we owe them.

To emphasize this point, Paul says to let no debt remain outstanding—that is, to let no debt go unpaid.

There's one exception, however. It's the debt of loving one another.

When we love others, we fulfill the law. This is because the singular instruction to love our neighbor as much as we love ourselves sums up all the commands of how to treat others.

Since God loved us so much, we should respond by loving one another as well (1 John 4:11).

Truly loving our neighbor means we do them no harm. In this way, love fulfills the law.

Loving God and loving others matters most.

How do we do at loving others as much as we love ourselves? What do we think about love being the fulfillment of the law? Is there anything else we should do that's not covered by the two greatest commandments of loving God and loving others?

[Discover more about loving others in Luke 6:31.]

DAY 33: BE CLOTHED WITH JESUS
ROMANS 13:11–14

Clothe yourselves with the Lord Jesus Christ, and do not think about how to gratify the desires of the flesh. (Romans 13:14)

Whether it's imminent or far away, each day takes us one day closer to the moment of Jesus's return and spending eternity with him. With this in mind, we should put aside all that is evil, that is, the deeds of darkness.

What is this evil? It's what occurs under the concealment of night. This covers carousing, drunkenness, sexual immorality, and debauchery. It even includes dissension and jealousy.

Instead of contemplating how to satisfy our sinful desires, we should clothe ourselves with Jesus. But what does it mean to clothe ourselves with our Savior?

From a spiritual sense, we remove what we're wearing—our old self—and put on fresh attire. As we follow Jesus, we strive to live like him. In this way, we clothe ourselves with Jesus, becoming more like him. In short, we wear Jesus.

The theological word for this is sanctification. This means we set ourselves apart for a special purpose, one holy and pure. Why do we do this? It isn't to earn our salvation. We can't do that. Our salvation comes through faith and believing in Jesus (Day 8). Instead, we choose to sanctify ourselves in response to what Jesus did for us. It's our way of saying thank you to him, of appreciating his greatest of all gifts—our eternal salvation.

In three of his other letters, Paul expands on what it means for us to clothe ourselves in Jesus.

First, in Galatians, Paul says that as God's children through faith, we were clothed with Jesus through our baptism (Galatians 3:26–28).

Recall that in Day 13 we said that baptism is a symbolic washing away of our sins to make us clean and justified before our Heavenly Father. It's also a powerful image that shows Jesus's death, burial, and resurrection: going into the water represents death, being submerged represents burial, and emerging from the water represents resurrection.

Through our baptism in Jesus, we take our first step to being clothed with him.

Second, to the Colossians, Paul writes that as God's chosen people, we're to clothe ourselves with compassion, kindness, humility, gentleness, and patience (Colossians 3:12). Don't rush past these five traits. Consider each one with careful attention. Then strive to make them a bigger part of your daily life.

Third, Paul says to clothe ourselves with what is imperishable and immortal. Through Jesus, we move from perishable to imperishable, mortality to immortality (1 Corinthians 15:53–54).

This means we need to change our perspective to align with our new standing through Jesus. We move our thinking from frail humanity to everlasting eternity.

In these ways we are clothed with Jesus.

What do we think about Paul's instructions to be clothed with Jesus? Are we becoming more like our Savior every day? If not, what must change?

[Discover being clothed with our heavenly dwelling in 2 Corinthians 5:2–4.]

BONUS CONTENT:
PUT ON THE ARMOR

Put on the armor of light. (Romans 13:12)

D oes the phrase *put on the armor* sound familiar? This isn't the only time Paul has used these words.

Yesterday's passage said that we are simply to put on the armor of light.

This carries a double meaning. The first is to move in the light of day and avoid those things done in the dark of night. The second meaning is to embrace the light of Jesus, as if wearing him as our attire.

In another of his letters, Paul tells us to put on the armor of God (Ephesians 6:11–18). With the image of a Roman soldier to guide us, we have the belt of truth, breastplate of righteousness, shoes of peace, shield of faith, helmet of salvation, and sword of the Spirit, which is the word of God.

Paul shares an alternate version of this in his letter to the Thessalonians. There he says to put on faith and love as a breastplate, along with our hope of salvation as a helmet (1 Thessalonians 5:8).

May we be mindful of these images when we rise each morning. As we prepare for the day by putting on our physical clothes, may we also put on our spiritual armor.

Which of these metaphors for our attire resonates most with us? How can these images impact how we go about our day as we live for Jesus?

[Discover more about Jesus's clothes in Matthew 17:2.]

DAY 34: LIVE FOR THE LORD

ROMANS 14:1–12

If we live, we live for the Lord; and if we die, we die for the Lord. So, whether we live or die, we belong to the Lord.

(Romans 14:8)

Throughout much of Romans 14, Paul discusses eating meat that was sacrificed to idols. Is it okay to partake, or is eating it a sin? After his opening discussion on the matter, Paul gives guidelines to help each person determine the right answer for him or her.

Amid his teaching, however, Paul slips in an overarching principle that should guide all that we do, say, and think.

In view of how we live our lives, we should live

for God. And when we die, we die for him. We belong to our Lord in both life and death. May this truth guide everything we do and say for every remaining moment we're alive.

As we live for our Lord, let us clothe ourselves with Jesus (Day 33). Let us put on his armor of light (Romans 13:12). In this way, we will become more like him, day by day, year by year.

Love is the key to guiding us in how to best do this. First, we love God. Next, we love others as much as we love ourselves (Day 32). If we focus on these two things, we effectively cover everything else.

Just as we live for our Lord, we die for our Lord. Whether our death is near or far away, let us remember this when we contemplate our end here on earth. May we finish strong.

In his letter to the Philippians, Paul gives his view on this when he says, "For to me, to live is Christ and to die is gain" (Philippians 1:21). What an impressive perspective to have. We live our lives not for our own comfort or in seeking our own good, but we live for Jesus.

Everything we do should be in response to what Jesus did to save us. We live for him, encouraging those who believe and serving as an inviting example to those who don't. This is our reason and purpose for living. May we never lose sight of this.

And when our life on this earth is over, our body dies. But this is even better. Through our physical death we gain life everlasting. May our death bring glory to God and point people to Jesus.

What should we do to better live for Jesus? What should we stop doing that hampers our living for him? When we die, how can we die for our Lord?

[Discover more about Paul's perspective on his own life in Acts 20:24 and 2 Timothy 4:7.]

BONUS CONTENT:
REGARDING THE DAYS

*One person considers one day more sacred than another;
another considers every day alike. Each of them should be
fully convinced in their own mind.* (Romans 14:5)

Amid Paul's teaching about eating meat sacrificed to idols, he slips in an example to illustrate a different way to consider this contentious issue. He talks about how we view each day.

Some consider special days to be sacred. This could include the Old Testament celebrations, as well as observing a weekly Sabbath. Other people, reasoning that Jesus came to show us a better way, set aside what the law teaches. They view each day as the same.

The purpose of Paul's illustration is to show that with disputable issues, each person should do what their conscience tells them. We should be fully convinced in our own minds of what to do or not do. Then we should stick to it. If we treat one day as special, we do so for God (Romans 14:6).

Though eating meat that was sacrificed to idols isn't something we face today, determining how to treat our Sabbath and our holidays is.

Whatever we decide on this matter, we should keep it between ourselves and God, who will bless us if we hold fast to what we have determined (Romans 14:22). We should align our actions with our beliefs (Romans 14:14).

If we judge the Sabbath day as sacred—be it on a Saturday or Sunday—we should not criticize those who do not (Colossians 2:16). Conversely, if we hold that the Sabbath is like all other days, we're wrong to encourage others to change their minds— that is, their convictions—to agree with us.

Whether on Saturday or Sunday, how do we view our

Sabbath? Are we holding to what our conscience tells us? Do we offer grace to those who hold the opposite view?

[Discover more about how to handle potentially contentious issues in 1 Corinthians 8:9 and 1 Corinthians 10:32–33.]

DAY 35: MAKE EVERY EFFORT
ROMANS 14:13–23

Let us therefore make every effort to do what leads to peace and to mutual edification. (Romans 14:19)

In summarizing his discussion about eating idol-sacrificed meat, Paul says to make every effort to do what leads to peace and to mutual satisfaction. This is a wise guideline that we can apply to any contentious issue we may face.

Today, we don't face the quandary of eating meat sacrificed to idols, but we do face other perplexing issues. These can cause disagreement between individuals, within local churches, at denominational levels, and beyond.

If we don't handle debatable matters properly,

these disputes escalate into conflict, which can cause division. These divisions dishonor God and thwart our witness. Instead, we should live as one, just as Jesus and his Father are one (John 17:20–23).

I once read about a church split that occurred several decades ago because of a disagreement over whether men should wear neckties to church services. Though this issue seems laughable to most of us today, I'm sure it seemed most serious to the people back then.

Instead of dividing over this issue, they should've followed Paul's advice to make every effort to live at peace and edify each other. When we face contentious issues today, may we avoid their error and follow Paul's prescription.

Let us always pursue peace. Peace is the absence of hostility. It emerges as a quiet calm. Achieving peace, however, requires both parties to want it. This is outside of our control; we cannot force another person to accept the peace we offer. What is within our control, however, is to pursue peace. We must, therefore, do whatever we can to pursue peace and then trust God with the rest.

We're to live at peace with everyone (Romans 12:18, 1 Corinthians 7:15, 1 Thessalonians 5:13, and Hebrews 12:14).

Likewise is mutual edification. Unlike peace—which we hear about often—edification isn't as common a term. Edification is the act of helping someone to improve themselves spiritually and morally. In a Christian context, edification helps others become more like Jesus.

Since Paul attaches the word *mutual* to the word *edification*, it's a reciprocal action, with us helping others and allowing them to help us. When we edify others, we build them up (1 Corinthians 14:26 and 1 Thessalonians 5:11). In this way, we encourage one another (2 Corinthians 13:11, 1 Thessalonians 4:18, and Hebrews 3:13).

Let us make every effort to do what leads to peace and mutual edification.

In what areas do we need to work harder to pursue peace? What can we do that leads to the edification of other believers? How can we let others edify us?

[Discover other areas where we should "make every effort" to do something in Luke 13:24, Ephesians 4:3, Hebrews 4:11, 2 Peter 1:5, 2 Peter 1:10, 2 Peter 1:15, and 2 Peter 3:14.]

DAY 36: ACCEPT ONE ANOTHER
ROMANS 15:1–13

Accept one another, then, just as Christ accepted you, in order to bring praise to God. (Romans 15:7)

Paul writes that we're to accept one another. This is easy to agree with in our minds, but it's harder to put into practice. Most people find it challenging to accept those different from themselves.

To give us clarity into how we should do this and why, Paul reminds us that Jesus accepts us—all of us. We aren't worthy of his acceptance. We can do nothing to earn it; our actions don't merit it. But Jesus accepts us just as we are, flaws and all. So, too, we should accept one another. If Jesus offers his acceptance of us, we can certainly do that for others.

When we accept others, as Jesus accepted us, the result brings praise to God. Our obedience to Paul's instruction to accept one another is one more way for us to worship our Heavenly Father.

In another of Paul's letters, he writes that we are all one in Jesus. In Jesus and through Jesus there is neither Jew nor Gentile, neither slave nor free, neither male nor female (Galatians 3:28). We're all one when we follow Jesus (Day 29).

Let's apply some of these ideas to our culture today.

Neither Jew nor Gentile: When we accept one another, we're not to make a distinction between Jew and Gentile. This has both ethnic and spiritual implications. First, it doesn't matter what race we are. We're to accept Jesus's followers from all races and all cultures.

Second, our spiritual background doesn't matter either. Some of us were raised by God-honoring parents and others weren't. But when we follow Jesus, our past isn't an issue. It also doesn't matter if we're evangelical or charismatic, prefer liturgy or not, or hold different views on the end times.

Neither Slave nor Free: Jesus's church in

Paul's day comprised both free people and slaves. Though slavery looked different then from how we understand it today, Paul says to accept them.

Today we might extend this to consider the type of work people do. There are professionals and laborers. There are white-collar and blue-collar. Then there are jobs that require a college education and those that don't. We should esteem all people who follow Jesus the same, regardless of the type of work they do—or how much they earn. We accept them all, mindful that Jesus accepts us.

Neither Male nor Female: This final pairing reminds us that in God's sight our gender doesn't matter. Remember that our Creator made us male and female in his image (Genesis 1:27). We're the same to God. We should, therefore, esteem all of Jesus's followers as the same, accepting them all, not making distinctions because they're male or female. (We'll cover this more in our upcoming bonus chapter, Women in Ministry.)

May we keep all these various people of Jesus's church in mind as we strive to accept one another just as Jesus accepts us.

Which group of people do we find it hard to embrace? Who are the individuals we struggle to accept? Why? How can we better move toward accepting others as Jesus accepts us?

[Discover more about accepting others in Romans 3:22–23, 1 Corinthians 12:13–14, and Colossians 3:11.]

DAY 37: CONVINCED

ROMANS 15:14–22

I myself am convinced, my brothers and sisters, that you yourselves are full of goodness, filled with knowledge and competent to instruct one another. (Romans 15:14)

Paul writes that he's convinced the people in the church in Rome possess three characteristics. We know Paul has never been to Rome at this point. We also see no hint he has received any direct input from others about what's happening there.

It's likely, therefore, that Paul's confidence in what he's about to say comes from the Holy Spirit. Though it's possible it applies only to the church in Rome, it may be a generic statement applying to all churches, that is, to all who follow Jesus.

First, Paul says he's convinced that they're full of goodness. Second, they're filled with knowledge. And third, they're competent to instruct one another. Let's focus on this last item: they're competent to instruct one another. Paul is convinced of this truth.

The attitude today at many churches, however, doesn't align with Paul's statement. Most people expect the professional clergy to teach them. These people assume it's their place to learn, not to teach others. But Paul sees (at least for the church in Rome) that they're competent to instruct one another. They don't need clergy or paid staff to do this. They should do it themselves.

We shouldn't be surprised, then, when Paul tells the people at another church to teach and admonish one another (Colossians 3:16). If the Roman and Colossian churches are supposed to instruct one another, why should we assume we aren't?

Peter is perhaps more pointed in this matter. He writes to the church at large that we are to become a holy priesthood (1 Peter 2:5). This is something to move toward. But a little later, he says we are a royal priesthood (1 Peter 2:9). That is, our status as priests has already occurred. It's a present reality, not a future aspiration.

What did the priests in the Old Testament do? They pointed the people to God and helped them connect with him. Though they too often fell short, they were intended to be God's liaisons with his people.

If we are a holy, royal priesthood—serving our Lord and Savior—we should follow the mission of the Old Testament priests. We should point people to God; we should help them connect with him. One essential way to do this is when we instruct one another.

And if we don't think we're ready for this, Paul thinks otherwise. In fact, he's convinced of it.

Do we expect our ministers and paid church staff to be the only ones to instruct us? What can we do to teach others? How might we go about doing this?

[Discover a church that may not be ready to instruct one another in 1 Corinthians 3:1–2.]

DAY 38: CARE FOR THE JEWS
ROMANS 15:23–33

For if the Gentiles have shared in the Jews' spiritual blessings, they owe it to the Jews to share with them their material blessings. (Romans 15:27)

P aul has written much about the Gentiles in his letter to the Romans; he's also talked about the Jews. More pointedly, he's addressed the relationship between the two groups.

Many Gentiles have turned to Jesus, but not as many Jews have. Paul makes it clear, however, that all who follow Jesus—both Jew and Gentile—are God's chosen people (Day 24).

The Jews approach God through the law, which points to the need for Jesus to save them. The

Gentiles, without the law to guide them, likewise need Jesus to save them (Days 6, 7, and 8). Though both groups approach Jesus from different perspectives, they likewise share the need to turn to him for salvation—to receive eternal life (Day 21).

The promise of salvation in the Old Testament is to the Jews. Notably, Jesus is Jewish. Gentiles who come to Jesus do so through the Jews' spiritual foundation.

In this way, Gentiles share in the Jews' spiritual blessings, as promised in the Old Testament. It's critical to note that Paul says they *share*. Gentiles have not displaced the Jews as God's chosen people. Both receive God's blessings through Jesus.

Because the Gentiles who align with Jesus receive their spiritual heritage from the Jews, they owe it to the Jews to give back to them; they can share their material blessings. The churches in Corinth and Galatia do just that (1 Corinthians 16:1–4).

When Paul writes his letter to the Romans, he's on his way to Jerusalem to deliver this money. It's helping Jesus's Jewish believers with their physical poverty.

When they turned to Jesus, the other Jews in Jerusalem likely ostracized them. This would make it more challenging for them to conduct trade and earn a living. They were struggling financially and needed help. We get a hint of this with the early church in Jerusalem when they worked to feed each other (Acts 6:1–7).

By extension today, when we see Jews who follow Jesus (sometimes called Messianic Jews) who struggle financially, we should help them however we can. We owe it to them. Paul says so.

Beyond this, however, we need to do whatever we can to help all other Jews turn to Jesus. This is so that all Israel will be saved (Romans 11:25–27).

Do we need to change anything in our attitude toward Jewish people? What can we do to help Messianic Jews who have material needs? What can we do to point all other Jews to Jesus?

[Discover more about what Paul has to say about Jews and Gentiles in 1 Corinthians 1:23, 1 Corinthians 12:13, 2 Corinthians 11:26, and Galatians 2:15–16.]

DAY 39: WATCH OUT
ROMANS 16:1–24

Watch out for those who cause divisions and put obstacles in your way that are contrary to the teaching you have learned. Keep away from them. (Romans 16:17)

I n the middle of Paul's long roster of people to greet and affirm, he interrupts his dictation to slip in some teaching. Since it doesn't seem connected with the text before or after it, it must be that this important instruction came to Paul as something essential to share. It seems he wanted to include it in his letter before he forgot.

He urges the recipients of his epistle to watch out for people who sow discord. They're also to watch out for people who wrongly add to what it means to follow Jesus. In both cases, Paul wants the believers to stay away from such people.

This instruction, however, isn't directed at divisive and legalistic people in the world; it's implicitly intended for those within our faith family. Therefore, in our church gathering, we must avoid people who create dissension, as well as those who devise unbiblical rules that they want everyone to follow.

These people—those who cause division and put hurdles in our path—are not serving the Lord. Instead, they're feeding their own appetites. Egotistically, they seek to elevate themselves to positions of power and authority. Using carefully crafted language, they deceive people who aren't careful about scrutinizing what they hear.

Paul also writes to the Corinthian church about the problem of discord. He tells them to agree with each other in what they say, to make sure there are no divisions among them. Instead, they should be perfectly united in what they believe and think (1 Corinthians 1:10).

Unfortunately, Paul later admits he has heard— and suspects it's true—that there are divisions among them (1 Corinthians 11:18). This may be why he teaches them about being part of the body (1 Corinthians 12:12–26). He also addresses this topic in his letter to the Romans, which we covered in Day 29.

As far as Paul's warning against those who put up obstacles, he doesn't address that in any of his other letters, but Isaiah does. He envisions a time when obstacles will be removed from the people's path (Isaiah 57:14).

Though Paul, like everyone else, is aware of the Roman church's obedience—and rejoices because of it—he still mentions his concern. He wants them to be wise about what is good and innocent about what is evil.

May we likewise be wise to what is good and right, focusing on it and avoiding evil with a child-like innocence. This includes uniting divisions and removing obstacles.

What can we do to heal division? What can we do to remove obstacles that hamper people from coming to Jesus or growing in their faith? How can we better be wise about what is good and right?

[Discover more about being wise in Proverbs 23:19, Daniel 12:3, and James 3:13.]

BONUS CONTENT: WOMEN IN MINISTRY

I commend to you our sister Phoebe, a deacon of the church in Cenchreae. (Romans 16:1)

Paul wraps up his letter to the Romans with a lengthy list of people to greet and affirm. Many of them are women, serving in various ministry roles. We can learn much from them.

He starts with Phoebe. She's a church deacon and a benefactor (Romans 16:1–2). This means she is both a leader and a generous person. Paul affirms her for that and asks the people in Rome to receive her in a worthy manner.

Next is Priscilla, along with her husband Aquila

(Romans 16:3–5). It's interesting that Paul, as well as Luke, often gives Priscilla first billing over her husband. Yet in other instances, we read Aquila's name first and then Priscilla. At the very least, this suggests they're coequals in their ministry. Yet this countercultural approach more likely means that Priscilla takes the lead in ministry and Aquila supports her. They risked their lives for Paul and have a church that meets in their home.

Next, Paul mentions Mary, noting she has worked very hard (Romans 16:6). There are many women in the New Testament named Mary, possibly as many as seven—all from Judea. This Mary could be one of them, who moved to Rome, or she could be another Mary. Regardless, she has a reputation for hard work.

Then we have Junia (Romans 16:7). Though Junia could be a male or female name, we can reasonably assume she's female and paired with her husband, Andronicus. Regardless, they're Jewish, standout apostles, followers of Jesus, and in prison, likely for their faith.

Tryphena and Tryphosa may be sisters, or they could be friends, but the key is they function well as a team. They work hard for the Lord (Romans 16:12).

Another hard worker is Persis, whom Paul calls a dear friend (Romans 16:12).

Next is Rufus's mother. She is like a mother to Paul (Romans 16:13).

Last, we have Julia, Nereus's sister, and Olympas (Romans 16:15). We don't know why Paul mentions these three women, but he feels it's important to do so. They know why. More importantly, God knows. That's what matters.

Regardless of our gender, these women in ministry can inspire us today.

We can be church leaders and generous bene-factors to missionaries. We can take a lead role in telling others about Jesus and opening our home for a house church. And whatever we do, we can work hard for the Lord. We can also be a mother (or parental figure) to others, be it spiritually or physi-cally. And we should be prepared to face persecu-tion for our faith, such as imprisonment.

The main point is that we do all we can to serve Jesus and grow the kingdom of God.

What else can we learn from these amazing women? How can they inspire us to do more for our Lord?

[Discover more about Priscilla and Aquila in Acts 18:1–3, Acts 18:18–20, Acts 18:24–26, 1 Corinthians 16:19, and 2 Timothy 4:19.]

[Read about these women and many, many more in Peter's book *Women of the Bible*.]

DAY 40: GLORY FOREVER
ROMANS 16:25–27

To the only wise God be glory forever through Jesus Christ!
Amen. (Romans 16:27)

P aul concludes his letter with a benediction (Romans 16:25–26). It opens with, "Now to him who is able to . . ." But what follows isn't a rousing inspiration that flows smoothly from our lips and sparks a stirring grandeur.

Instead, it's a series of deep theological phrases that don't flow forth with ease. Rather, we're confronted with a decision. Do we gloss over these two verses, or do we spend time in contemplation? Let's take a moment to dig into it.

First, the blessing is to God. He saves us through the good news of Jesus. It's a message that Paul proclaims. This message aligns with a mysterious revelation hidden from long ago (Ephesians 3:8–9). It began before the creation of our world (1 Corinthians 2:7).

What is this mystery? Good question.

Aside from the mysteries mentioned in the books of Daniel and Revelation, Paul is the only other biblical writer to talk about mystery. He does this often. Yet he seems to reference multiple mysteries. The most likely mystery is that the promised Messiah will come to save Gentiles—and not just the Jews (Ephesians 3:6).

Though this mystery is revealed now through Jesus, the prophets foresaw long ago that God would save the nations, that is, the Gentiles (Psalm 22:27, Isaiah 42:6, Isaiah 49:6, Jeremiah 16:19, and Malachi 1:11).

The result of all this—God's plan from before creation, the prophets' proclamations, and Jesus's saving work—is that the Gentiles can come to obedience through faith (Day 22 and Romans 10:10, Hebrews 10:39, and James 2:14).

Having proclaimed all this, we expect Paul to end with a hearty amen. He does not. Instead, he seems to regroup, aware that he has just packed a benediction with deep theological thought.

Paul now takes a step back in his dictation. He seems to start his benediction anew. This time he simply proclaims: "To the only wise God be glory forever through Jesus Christ!"

To confirm he's done this time, he ends with "Amen."

In this, Paul declares that God is the only wise God. We give him eternal glory. We do this through Jesus Christ. So be it!

When we encounter confusing Bible passages, do we rush through them or slow down to contemplate them? Do we fully embrace the truth that God is the only wise God? How well do we do at giving glory to God through Jesus Christ?

[Discover some of Paul's other mentions of mystery in 1 Corinthians 15:51–52, Ephesians 1:7–10, Colossians 1:25–27, Colossians 2:2, Colossians 4:3, and 1 Timothy 3:16.]

If you liked *Romans Bible Study,* please leave a review online. Your review will help others discover this book and encourage them to read it too.

Thank you.

BOOKS IN THE 40-DAY
BIBLE STUDY SERIES

Which book do you want to read next in the 40-Day Bible Study Series?

Dear Theophilus (the Gospel of Luke)

Acts Bible Study

Isaiah Bible Study

Minor Prophets Bible Study

Job Bible Study

Living Water (John)

Love Is Patient (1 and 2 Corinthians)

Revelation Bible Study

1, 2, & 3 John Bible Study

Hebrews Bible Study

James and Jude Bible Study

Matthew Bible Study

1 & 2 Peter Bible Study

Mark Bible Study

FOR SMALL GROUPS, SUNDAY SCHOOL, AND CLASSES

Romans Bible Study makes an ideal eight-week Bible study discussion guide for small groups, Sunday School, and classes. To prepare for the conversation, read one chapter of this book each weekday, Monday through Friday.

- Week 1: read 1 through 5.
- Week 2: read 6 through 10.
- Week 3: read 11 through 15.
- Week 4: read 16 through 20.
- Week 5: read 21 through 25.
- Week 6: read 26 through 30.
- Week 7: read 31 through 35.
- Week 8: read 36 through 40.

When you get together, discuss the questions at the end of each chapter. The leader can use all the questions to guide your discussion or pick which ones to focus on.

Before you begin, pray as a group. Ask for Holy Spirit insight and clarity.

As you consider each chapter's questions:

- Look at how this can grow your understanding of the Bible.
- Evaluate how this can expand your faith perspective.
- Consider what you need to change in how you live your lives.

End by asking God to help apply what you've learned.

May God bless you as you read and study his Word.

IF YOU'RE NEW TO THE BIBLE

Each entry in this book contains Bible references. These can guide you if you want to learn more. If you're not familiar with the Bible, here's an overview to get you started, give some context, and minimize confusion.

First, the Bible is a collection of works written by various authors over several centuries. Think of the Bible as a diverse anthology of godly communication. It contains historical accounts, poetry, songs, letters of instruction and encouragement, messages from God sent through his representatives, and prophecies.

Most versions of the Bible have sixty-six books grouped into two sections: the Old Testament and the New Testament. The Old Testament contains thirty-nine books that precede and anticipate Jesus. The New Testament includes twenty-seven books and covers Jesus's life and the work of his followers.

The reference notations in the Bible, such as Romans 3:23, are analogous to line numbers in a Shakespearean play. They serve as a study aid. Since the Bible is much longer and more complex than a play, its reference notations are more involved.

As already mentioned, the Bible is an amalgam of books, or sections, such as Genesis, Psalms, or Matthew. These are the names given to them, over time, based on the piece's author, audience, or purpose.

In the 1200s, each book was divided into chapters, such as Acts 2 or Psalm 23. In the 1500s, the chapters were further subdivided into verses, such as John 3:16. Let's use this as an example.

The name of the book (John) appears first, followed by the chapter number (3), a colon, and then the verse number (16). Sometimes called a chapter-verse reference notation, this helps people quickly find a specific text regardless of their version of the Bible.

Although the goal was to place these chapter and verse divisions at logical breaks, they sometimes seem arbitrary. Therefore, it's good practice to read what precedes and follows each passage you're studying. The text before or after it may contain relevant insights into the portion you're exploring.

Here's how to look up a specific passage in the Bible based on its reference: Most Bibles contain a table of contents, which gives the page number for the beginning of each book. Start there. Locate the book you want to read, and turn to that page. Then flip forward to the chapter you want. Last, skim that chapter to locate the specific verse.

If you want to read online, enter the reference into BibleGateway.com or BibleHub.com. Also check out the YouVersion app.

Learn more about the greatest book ever written at ABibleADay.com, which provides a Bible blog, summaries of the books of the Bible, a dictionary of Bible terms, Bible reading plans, and other resources.

ABOUT PETER DEHAAN

Peter DeHaan, PhD, wants to change the world one word at a time. His books and blog posts discuss God, the Bible, and church, geared toward spiritual seekers and church dropouts. Many people feel church has let them down, and Peter seeks to encourage them as they search for a place to belong.

But he's not afraid to ask tough questions or make religious people squirm. He's not trying to be provocative. Instead, he seeks truth, even if it makes people uncomfortable. Peter urges Christians to push past the status quo and reexamine how they practice their faith in every part of their lives.

Peter earned his doctorate, awarded with high distinction, from Trinity College of the Bible and Theological Seminary. He lives with his wife in beautiful Southwest Michigan and wrangles crossword puzzles in his spare time.

A lifelong student of Scripture, Peter wrote the 1,000-page website ABibleADay.com to encourage people to explore the Bible, the greatest book ever written. His popular blog, at PeterDeHaan.com, addresses biblical Christianity to build a faith that matters.

Read his blog, receive his newsletter, and learn more at PeterDeHaan.com.

BOOKS BY PETER DEHAAN

40-DAY BIBLE STUDY SERIES

Dear Theophilus (the Gospel of Luke)

Acts Bible Study

Isaiah Bible Study

Minor Prophets Bible Study

Job Bible Study

Living Water (John)

Love Is Patient (1 and 2 Corinthians)

Revelation Bible Study

1, 2, & 3 John Bible Study

Hebrews Bible Study

James and Jude Bible Study

Matthew Bible Study

1 & 2 Peter Bible Study

Mark Bible Study

HOLIDAY CELEBRATION DEVOTIONALS

The Advent of Jesus

The Passion of Jesus (Lent)

The Victory of Jesus (Easter)

The Ministry of Jesus

Thanksgiving with Jesus

New Year with Jesus

BIBLE CHARACTER SKETCHES SERIES

Women of the Bible

The Friends and Foes of Jesus

Old Testament Sinners and Saints

More Old Testament Sinners and Saints

Heroes and Heavies of the Apocrypha

200 Old Testament Sinners and Saints

VISITING CHURCHES SERIES

52 Churches

The 52 Churches Workbook

More Than 52 Churches

The More Than 52 Churches Workbook

Visiting Online Church

Shopping for Church

OTHER BOOKS

Elephant God

Jesus's Broken Church

Martin Luther's 95 Theses (formerly *95 Tweets*)

The Christian Church's LGBTQ Failure

Bridging the Sacred-Secular Divide (formerly *Woodpecker Wars*)

Beyond Psalm 150

For the latest list of all Peter's books, go to PeterDeHaan.com/nonfiction.

www.ingramcontent.com/pod-product-compliance
Lightning Source LLC
Chambersburg PA
CBHW060517130626
46553CB00002B/529